RHIZODONT

KATRINA PORTEOUS

RHIZODONT

BLOODAXE BOOKS

ISBN: 978 1 78037 713 1

First published 2024 by
Bloodaxe Books Ltd,
Eastburn,
South Park,
Hexham,
Northumberland NE46 1BS.

www.bloodaxebooks.com
For further information about Bloodaxe titles
please visit our website or write to
the above address for a catalogue.

Supported using public funding by
**ARTS COUNCIL
ENGLAND**

Cover design: Neil Astley & Pamela Robertson-Pearce.

Printed in Great Britain by Bell & Bain Limited, Glasgow, Scotland, on
acid-free paper sourced from mills with FSC chain of custody certification.

CONTENTS

BOOK II: INVISIBLE EVERYWHERE

INTRODUCTION

The poems in *Rhizodont* fall into two distinct 'Books'. The first is a journey through the sedimentary landscapes of England's North-East coast. The poems begin in the former coalmining communities of East Durham, where my grandfather was a pitman, and travel north, to the shores of Northumberland just south of Berwick-upon-Tweed. Along the way they explore places and communities in transformation: the mouth of the Tyne, the former coal port of Amble, and the fishing and former quarrying and lime-burning settlements of Beadnell and Holy Island. The poems consider these places against a backdrop of geological time.

The 'rhizodont' of the title, whose name means 'rooted teeth', was a fearsome three-metre-long predatory fish which first appeared around 377 million years ago and became extinct 310 million years ago. A creature of swampy lakes, it belonged to a family of lobe-finned fishes which are the ancestors of all four-limbed vertebrates, including humans. The lobe-finned fishes' transition from water to land was one of the most significant events in vertebrate evolution. A rhizodont's fossil has been found in Carboniferous strata from around 330 million years ago at Cocklawburn on the Northumberland coast.

In comparison with the rhizodont's timescale, human history and prehistory occupy a mere few hundred thousand years. Even during human time, Earth's climate has fluctuated hugely. Only 15,000 years ago, all the landscapes of Book I were still locked under the ice of the most recent glacial period. In recent centuries, human activity on this coast has been driven by its geology, in particular by the extraction of coal, the fossil which fuelled the Industrial Revolution. Coal was laid down during the Carboniferous Period, 359-299 million years ago. On the East Durham coast the coal-bearing strata are overlain by younger rock. North of the Tyne, the Carboniferous strata are exposed at the surface. Coalmining and burning, and the recent demise of that industry, have had an enormous impact, not only on the landscape and wider environment, but on the way that we think about place, community and ecology.

The poems in Book I explore this broad sweep of time, and the changing cultures of each of these places, with close attention to the small and the local. Many of them focus on creatures which evolved many millions of years before humans, and which have accompanied us throughout our history, such as particular species of bird, insect, or plant life. The poems are arranged in sequences, some quite loosely connected; others, like 'A Lang Way Hyem' and 'The Long Line', are single long poems.

At first glance the poems in Book II appear quite different. This section, arranged around two long sequences written in collaboration with scientists, considers aspects of the latest waves of industrial and technological revolution. Rather than focusing on alternative energy sources to replace fossil fuels, they consider technologies which extend human senses and reasoning in completely new ways.

The first sequence, 'Ingenious', explores the remote sensing techniques, robotics and autonomous systems which allow humans to interact with hazardous environments, from nuclear waste storage facilities to other planets. These poems consider the implications of data-based technologies and artificial intelligence, and the understanding of complex systems, as new ways of thinking about the Earth and its ecology. Human consciousness is the most complicated system we know of in the Universe. It may be unique. Scientists have engineered machine learning and creativity, but not yet machine consciousness. Whether, when and how that might emerge is a matter of intense debate. 'Ingenious' considers aspects of this transformative moment.

The closing sequence, 'Under the Ice', focuses on the most inaccessible reaches of our planet, Antarctica, and the unseen worlds beneath its miles-deep ice. These poems explore in detail how the same remote sensing technologies and data analysis are used to understand more about our planet's systems, in particular its climate, and its patterns of change.

While the poems in these two sequences explore scientists' work, they are no more than a poet's response. I have no scientific background. I think of them, and the accompanying notes at the end of the book, as a heuristic device, a provocation to the reader to discover more and to reflect further.

Interspersed throughout both Books of *Rhizodont* is a group of linked poems from an audio sequence entitled 'Susurrations of the Sea'. These poems reflect on aspects of the role that oceans play in the evolution of Life, the deposition and erosion of rock, the 'carbon cycle', deep ocean currents, and the regulation of Earth's climate. Among their many functions, the oceans act as a carbon 'sink', absorbing excess energy, as carbon dioxide dissolves in water, causing them to become more acidic. Secondly, over enormous periods of geological time, the oceans also help to lock up some carbon dioxide in rock. Carboniferous limestone, composed of calcium, carbon and oxygen as calcium carbonate, was largely created from the shells and skeletons of marine creatures such as corals from a former world. These 'sea poems', which appear on pages 13, 14, 53, 96-7 and 112, touch lightly on these immense processes, and are intended as a kind of chorus, in conversation with the poems of both Books.

In the background to all the poems in *Rhizodont* is the notion that the generation born in the decades immediately after World War II occupies a unique place in history, straddling the transformation from analogue to digital technologies. Like the lobe-finned fishes, we have crawled from one 'world' into another. Some of the poems touch on one aspect of this transition, deindustrialisation. Others suggest that, for some, there has been a reduction in immediate physical exposure to certain experiences through the senses: think of children who watch film of whales on their phones but have never seen a stickleback in a rock pool, or adults who cycle for miles in a gym but rarely walk their local footpaths. At the same time, as the poems in Book II suggest, the senses are mediated and extended as never before, in science and industry through remote sensing technologies, and in everyday life, through live streaming, social networks, and 'virtual realities' experienced on a screen. So at different scales the poems in *Rhizodont* explore these changes, by which – like living creatures – communities, languages and cultures may flourish, evolve or become extinct.

Crucially, the rhizodont's fate reminds us that we are living at a time of biological mass extinction. Increasing computational power allows a growing understanding of the impact of our own proliferating species on the planet. The increasing human population seems paradoxically ever more threatening and ever more fragile, simultaneously impacting all too heavily upon the planet's processes, insignificant before them, and adaptive to them.

These poems invite us to think of human activity, not as separate from nature but as entirely part of it, a catalytic force – perhaps one that will be powerfully augmented by generative A.I. While fearfully destructive to the world of which it is part, human activity is defined by language and imagination, which the poems suggest may be seen as aspects of Life's astonishing powers of reinvention. Together, the poems of *Rhizodont* invite us to consider how social structures of language, creativity, science and imagination interact with nature's systems in networked 'feedback loops', enabling us, at our best, to understand, respond to and collaborate with the planet's processes in positive and life-giving ways.

KATRINA PORTEOUS

How the Fishes Listen

How many tens of million
Turns of a planet
Around its star before

It rolls out an instrument
To oscillate and shimmer
Out of phase with water?

In cavernous, internal
Ancestral seas, the countless
Grains of limestone shiver.

Otoliths. Cilia,
Kelp frond from holdfast,
Waft, invisible,

While the fishes listen –

Lobe-finned, or eyeless,
Catch the sea's quiver
Seething with violence

And fresh threat. Relic
Gill and spiracle,
Breathed out through us

From deepest oceanic
Darkness, into sparkling
Beach light, translate

Every sea-cave pulse,
Ripple, oscillation,
As place, direction, danger.

Ingredients

When you crunch your footprint
Into sand, or splash
Among the chill pools, chasing

Tiny sparks that dart
Under the cleft rock, listening
To the waves' slow wash,

Can you hear the distant
Rumble prising
Continents apart?

Every wave contains an imprint,
An echo of the last,
Of the next, a foretaste –

The hiss and fizz of heat.
Slowly an ocean
Swallows it. An engine

Scrambles ingredients
For spores, spines, fins, scales, bones,
From mineral, or ice.

Can you hear its pulse
In the deep roar, its ceaseless
Boom and bass?

BOOK I

CARBONIFEROUS

Tinkers' Fires

When I was a child I loved to play in the ashes of tinkers' fires. Inscrutable abandoned trinkets, treasure of old nails beautiful in their purple rust, fragile, crumbling in my fingers, they were holy relics, riddles in horseshoe heel-plate, D-rings, buckles, conjuring the sour dust of sweat, hoofbeat, harness races from the blue-black cinders. Sometimes a mud-caked pony chained to a stake grazed forlornly nearby. Be careful, Geordie Whittle said, pissing into the ashes so I would not burn myself. Muggers, flee-b'-neets, taggarine men and their women. We scarcely saw them. Their glamorous residues glowed in the embers. From the bruise-red pit-brick end of the colliery row, the cold, charred circle of their fires became a mystery I longed to enter; out of which I summoned, like a cave-painter, in charcoal and ochre, the hot dung smell, the hoofprint, of whatever is ephemeral, fugitive, itinerant, just passing through.

Tinkers: this word was used in Co Durham in the 1960s for travelling people who specialised in mending pots and pans. Today some people find it offensive. It is used here for historical reasons alongside other terms from the local dialect which might cause offence today; *muggers*: travelling people who sold earthenware pots; *flee-b'-neets:* itinerant horse-sellers who absconded at night; *taggarine men:* collectors of scrap iron; rag-and-bone men.

Kittycouldhavebeen

Kitty could have been a film-star. Born between the Wars
Between the narrow bedroom walls of a soot-black colliery row,
Coal smoke choking the summer air,

Pretty-as-a-picture. Everybody said so.
Sharp as a pin in her mother's pincushion, bright
As a button in her jar,

Smart as a sherbet dip, as the dangerous lipstick
She practised her signature with, the grammar school
Three miles over the fields, too far to travel.

Sixteen, expecting. The pit wheel, spinning. In the movie
That should have been Kitty's, after the War
Cracked open the chintzy bedrooms, shockingly naked

Hearths blazing with fireweed, Kitty could have been.
But no one owns a telephone, a car,
And the bus to Durham

Left over an hour ago, and there are floors to clean,
Pots to wash, sheets to peg out. Down the burn
Hawthorn is springing into blossom and the sedge is green,

And Kitty's son,
Never-born-right, never walked, heavy as a millstone,
Has never seen light; and the baby girl is laughing again,

Pretty hair plaited, dressed to the keel,
Not cornered by circumstance and sex.
Not trapped in the upstairs room by the shocking blaze that killed her.

The film reel spins in the dark. Pigeons wheel over Margaret Street;
Turn, a tight circle, home to the cree.
Whatever Kitty could have been,

The gods of history have forgiven her
Everything. Her great-great-granddaughter
Stubs out her cigarette on the steps of the boarded-up cinema.

Tiny Lights

At the edge of the industrial estate,
Fierce spikes fencing the weed strewn pit site,
A fly-tipped sofa, black sacks spilling

Paint cans and polythene,
We found it – the track –
And followed it down the millennia, into the Dene,

Where we waited, like brigands, for the dark,
And after a long while, you saw it first,
Hanging from a grass-stalk –

Greenish-white, faintly aglow,
Mysterious in the twenty-first century – alien, ancient.
We drowned its ghostly signal with the beams of our phones

And a torrent of information, explaining
How oxygen binds to a chemical, luciferin,
And how its hideous, segmented, armoured offspring

Paralyse snails and suck them out of their shells.
Not a mile away, a police siren wailed.
This wingless female,

Barely a glimmer in the cool, damp, scented night,
Seemed to have hauled itself
Up a long, long path –

From the remotest deep, the prehistoric
Ocean teeming with miraculous, barbaric
Creatures of dark places that emit their own light –

And we with it.

Wildlife

I *Lee*

Lee loves to play in the Dene. From a green flush
A wren is singing. 'The V' is a swamp,
Seething with prehistoric creatures. Dragonflies flash

Their glassy emeralds. Lee stirs the mud with a stick.
Tadpoles, beetles, scatter in alarm.
Lee likes to trot the wild-eyed ponies bareback

Over the pit site. A dumped fridge-freezer towers,
Its door wide open, clean lines, shelves intact.
Lee can't read what his friend's Dad posts on Facebook –

'Horden's answer to Easington's Pit Cage.' Aged nine,
Can't write his name, but knows the woodpeckers
By theirs; loves hedgehogs; wants to join the Army.

II *Lloyd*

Lloyd dreams of becoming an astronaut. At night,
He looks at the stars above the Numbered Streets,

Smashed glass, boarded-up windows: can't understand
How space is infinite, but everything ends.

He can't find words for all the contradictions.
The neat houses, 'respectable people', tidy gardens –

Lloyd thinks about these things. His caterpillar
Wrapped itself into a papery chrysalis; weeks later,

Shook out its flickering wings and flew. His Gran
Grew up on the same street, in a different country.

III *Kayleigh*

It's a short bike ride from the pit. Though the weeds conceal
Aerosols, glue cans, plastic bags, and in the Gill
Somebody's big sister is being sick beside a burned-out car,

On Limekiln Beach, among the remains of coal,
You can run and run, dig and build – make fires, feel free –
Crack the sea-smoothed rocks wide open to reveal

Fossils, crystals, caves of gleaming fluorspar.
And though the beach is brassy with pyrites, sulphurous, stained,
Deranged from everything it's seen, for Kayleigh the future

Glitters. She loves this place; and with her friends
Seeks out the scuttling hermit crabs, crimson anemones.
The dazed beach offers them its treasures. What will they find?

Coastal Erosion

First to go is the footpath, smoking fireweed, the hawthorn
Reddening along the Grassy Banks; then the railway line,
The end terraces, blackened memorials –

Pit cage and pulley wheel, small family shrines,
Allotments, community centres. Then the words for these things –

Bairns, Flower, Hinny, me Marra. Reminders
That what will survive of us is not love but chip forks,
Booty that Liam and Reece grab on their Pirate Litter-Pick –

Bottle tops, take-away cartons, lids, straws, nappy-liners,
Carrier bags, falling apart into ever-smaller pieces,

Accreting down there on the beach, while a limp balloon
Snagged on the whin's thorn, indestructible plastic
Printed with soon-to-be incomprehensible runes,

Announces to no one, 'Baby! I love you!'

Bairns: children; *Flower, Hinny:* two terms of endearment; *Marra:* mate.
In mining, your marra was your working partner; *whin:* gorse.

A Short Walk from the Sea's Edge

'The Sea is History'

DEREK WALCOTT

'The coal is beginning again'

SEAN O'BRIEN
('Fantasia on a Theme of James Wright')

Our Billy's Da walks the dog on the Grassy Banks each morning.
Seventy steps below, in the soft ochre shelf,
Each new tide kirves its jud. Its strata an archive,
The beach is forgetting itself.

The coast path tells one story, and the shore another.
A steep drop, headlong, precipitous. Inaccessible, inviting,
The sea rolls its old stones, stained fiery amber. 'Once
The worst pollution anywhere in Europe,' boasts the sign.

Now hogweed and scrub willow are slowly erasing that hard-drive;
Shales, pyrites, oxides, remember hermit crabs, rock pools.
Inland, behind the railway line, our Billy's granddaughter,
Chloe, checks in with Insta before school.

Our Billy's Chloe has no word for bluebell or cowslip,
Willow or yellowhammer. Granda's pigeons wheel and turn
Over the tracks, but she doesn't know *stobbie* from *skyemmie*.
A soft breeze blows from the beach. A smell of burning.

Lads on their dirt-bikes down the slacks. Amid the limestone rubble,
Tall reeds, rushes, someone has tried to set that sign alight,
Photographs of butterflies, orchids, twisted, distorted.
Half a mile from the coast, impenetrably tight,

The roofs, rows, back lanes – safety. Chloe has a butterfly
Emoji glued to every nail. Her own words – *Gels, Acrylics, Apps* –
Incomprehensible to Billy's ears, are strange, untranslatable
As *yella-yowlie, gowdspink* are on Snapchat.

The old words clatter off men's lips: honeycombs of tree-bark
And giant ferns, frozen in mudstone, sinking into slag
In the relentless crunch and uproar of immense machinery –
Canch, post, rammel. NCB. The Low Main. Maggie. Scab.

Beyond them, wordless, stretch the fields, the sea. Glued to her phone,
Chloe waits at the bus-stop on the Coast Road, at the edge of the Dene
Where, among sparty ground, green seggs, gigantic ferns
And spidery horsetails, the coal is beginning again.

kirve a jud: in mining, to undercut a section of coal before taking it down; *stobbie:*
unfledged pigeon; *skyemmie:* weak, sickly pigeon; *yella-yowlie:* yellowhammer;
gowdspink: goldfinch; *canch:* large slabs of stone removed from a coalmine to make
space; *post:* hard sandstone; *rammel:* loose stones; *NCB:* the National Coal Board,
the statutory authority which ran the nationalised coal industry from 1946 until
its demise in 1987; *The Low Main:* one of the deep seams worked at Horden pit;
Maggie: Margaret Thatcher, Prime Minister at the time of the 1984-85 miners'
strike and subsequent pit closures; *scab:* a strike-breaker; *sparty:* damp, marshy;
seggs: sedge and rushes.

Painted Ladies

Although she would never normally set foot
Beyond the railway line, because the beach is dirty,
Her Mam said; spoilt before she was born, rust-stained and orange,

Black with slag and dolly-wash, its terrible lagoons
Haemorrhaging sulphates, oxides – some ancient outrage
No one alive can remember now – Leanne sets out

Down her Granda's red-black raa' – path of putter and hewer,
Backshift, foreshift; pigeon cree; policeman and picket –
With his bairn in a Tupperware box. Up the White Lea lane,

Through fireweed and meadow grass, she wades, to the brink –
To the windy cliff at Shippersea, the clean horizon.
In a handful of ashes she brings her Mam to beauty.

Then far below, incarnadine, ochre, black, white
Pigments of caustic pools and residues, fly up, combine –
Embers, aflame inside, aglow in the grate,

Flickering from knapweed to thistle-top, they rise
Blazing before her – butterflies – the fields
From Hawthorn Hive to Eden Dene on fire with them.

dolly-wash: water containing coal dust and chemicals leached from pit; *raa':*
row (of houses); *putter:* pitman who pushed the tubs of coal from the coal
face; *hewer:* pitman who cut coal; *cree:* coop.

Speckled Wood

Holly has found a butterfly
In Hawthorn Dene. The Brownies
Have been given cameras.

Framed in the viewfinder,
Its drab brown colours
Spring to life: snap

Into focus, coffee and toast,
Caramel, splotches of cream,
Smoke rings. Scalloped like bunting,

Its edges bristle with hairs.
What Holly, aged nine,
Can't know, is that it has come back

From wherever it has been,
In the new millennium, to say
It is warmer here now.

Don't move, thinks Holly,
Though whether to herself
Or the butterfly, she isn't sure.

The camera is showing her
What her eyes can't –
How to look. How, when you're still

And quiet, the world
Rises anew
To meet you, shining.

Hermeneutics

Out you go, my great-grandmother, never owned a coat
Because you never travelled far enough to need one.
And my mother's mother, out

From kale-pot and pit-yacker shop: slag-heap, coal reek, soot.
What would you have made of my books,
My Northern granddams, my tough-knuckled pioneers?

No one likes a clever-clogs. A back-chatter. A sharp-tongued chit
Stepping off a train, unchaining her bicycle. Monastic lamplight
Pools on the flagstones at the bottom of D staircase

Where her name is inscribed. Where news arrives by pigeonhole
In a courtyard ablaze with geraniums, wisteria, difficult ideas
Contained within formal lineaments. Who will translate

A letter to my old tribe, my armies of dazzling brothers?
Under Garret Hostel Bridge slides the oil-black river.
A rustle like sparrows in the library's climbing roses.

Out you go, my granddaughters, knowing nothing
Of the yellowing novelties of forty years ago. Spinsters,
Career Girls, Gentlemen's Agreements. What did they mean?

Like index cards, and weeping into payphones,
The narrow, the analogue island we lived on
Shall be Latin and Greek to you, Ancient Phoenician.

Wooden Doll

Set her up high, the stem-head of the collier brig.
As if a woman were a ship
Bearing her human cargo like a caryatid,

Silent as oak beneath the adze, and stoic,
Freighted with virtue, she will ride
Before us like the eyes of a Phoenician galley, old as trade.

Sail-maker, block and mast-maker, blacksmith of Liddell Street –
Make me a skillet, a swull, a creel for your back.
As if a woman were an empty vessel

Brimming with meanings like a pewter pot,
Stop her mouth with salt, with Nancy Bothwick's stout –
Fine codlin's, hinny, cheaper than butcher's meat –

That everything done to her may be forgiven.
So like a capstan, she might bide. As if the word Woman
Carried its burden, shifting its bearings, fluent as silt

Drifting softly past the Worm Beds on the silent
Tide, beyond the Mussel Scarp, the Black Middens –
Till some current whirls it, out, to the horizon.

Saa't

Mother packed up aal hor rough love
Amang the pinafores. Aah can mind hor yet,
Reed–raa' fing'ers tyin' me kist. Aah'd nivvor been away afore.
Ye canna keep ahaa'd on a slippery harrin'.

W' landed amang the keelboats' clatter, yon fresh smell clean
On the wund's knife. Sill'er heaped i' the farlins,
Wor Cooper teemin' 'em oot like rain. Nettie, Nellie, an' me
Sixteen year aa'd that summer. We shuggled on wor bamskins,

Cloots on wor fing'ers, the torn floor bags,
Cotton i' wor mooth. An' wha larned us
Hoo t' tie 'em aroond an' aroond? Airm in airm, an' laughin',
Aa' hookit togither like a raa' a knittin'

W' clattered doon Main Street at forst light; aye, an' often
It was efter midnight afore w' saw wor beds agyen,
Sair backs, bobbin' up an doon; wi' me fower tubs, packin'.
Ha' ye cracked a barr'l open? Them black backs come up lovely,

Heed t' heed an' tail t' tail, bright as the new shillin's
W' fetched back t' wor Mams. Reed airms i' the roosin' tub,
Clickety–clack on the wet flags – varnigh a machine,
Thoosands on thoosands a harrin' cleaned in twa dabs,

Till we telt w' Smaa' for' w' Matt-full by the sheer feel on it.
By the silk on a harrin' an' the sting a saa't we wore made women,
Larned wor rough love, airm in airm, clatterin' doon the lonnen,
Laughin', aa' t'githor, strang as ony man.

Saa't: salt, shorthand for salt herring. Unmarried girls from the NE coast 'followed the fishing' in the early 20th century, travelling south with the herring shoals to process the catch in teams; *kist:* a wooden chest (girls following the fishing carried their belongings in a kist); *farlins:* troughs in which herring were sorted; *Cooper:* overseer of herring yard; *bamskins:* oilskin aprons; *cloots:* rags (tied with cotton to protect fingers); *roosin':* roughly salting; *Smaa':* small herring; *Matt-full:* herring full of milt or roe, not less than nine and a quarter inches long; *lonnen:* lane.

Low Light

Raffle for the Fishermen, raffle for the Mission,
Go down, Old Low Light.
Everybody here has someone missing.
Low Light, go down.

In the bustle of the boxes on the pallets on the Quay
Go down, Old Low Light,
A woman on deck gonna vex the sea.
Low Light, go down.

Granddad ring-netted out of Oban.
Go down, Old Low Light.
Wouldn't take me with him till I learnt to tie a bowline.
Low Light, go down.

Tommy Scorer showed me the scene,
Go down, Old Low Light.
Towin' for sprats on the Girl Irene.
Low Light, go down.

Followed the ice to the Northern cod,
Go down, Old Low Light.
Irvin's 'Ben' Boats next to God.
Low Light, go down.

Tied up the boat at the Knuckle End,
Go down, Old Low Light,
Shovellin' prawns with the best of men.
Low Light, go down.

It's a hard, hard life, chewin' oot the Gut.
Go down, Old Low Light.
A pan of shackles may be all ye'll get.
Low Light, go down.

Knackered, askin' – Why d' ye take it?
Go down, Old Low Light.
Tight as family. Can't escape it.
Low Light, go down.

Never saved nothin' for a rainy day,
Go down, Old Low Light.
Never had much gives most away.
Low Light, go down.

Harry says, when it come coarse weather
Go down, Old Low Light,
The rogues an' the angels sing together.
Low Light, go down.

Raffle for the Lifeboat, raffle for the Mission,
Go down, Old Low Light.
Everybody here got someone missing.
Low Light, go down.

Go down, Old Low Light,
Low Light, go down.

Shields Gut

The men in yellow oilskins want to know why
They have grown old shovelling tonne after tonne of cod
Into the bellies of gannets for no reason.
Moored near the gun embrasures, inland of Collingwood,

They work among rust and oak, the Dutch, French and Spanish,
Flickering U-boat and sweeper, receding out of sight.
Did nobody hear them in their silent newsreel, smoky drifters
Fading into stuttering black and white?

But here they are still, the prawn fleet, flying the flag.
The skipper's explaining to a TV crew, the sea is a garden.
Fixed Quota Allocation Units won't rhyme with that.
Keep what ye catch, and limit the days ye gan

And gi' us back control over wor own waters.
Behind him, a Tapas Bar. His crew's Filipino, his market's France,
The kittiwakes argue the water's theirs, and the tide brings more plastic.
The future opens its phrasebook. Who should we ask

If those stone piers curve towards Europe? The sea is a road.
Somewhere out there is a life-raft, full of frightened people
Fleeing the world's cruelty. Sea of plenty,
Sea of hunger, we are those people.

Passage Migrants

It has taken a long time
To reach here – countless

Wing-beats, a hunger
To go, without knowing where.

Each time, the same –
Desolate, the tundra.

Stint, sandpiper, rising.
Deserts to cross. Between,

This precise place:
The Pleistocene shore,

Stitched with worm,
Riveted with barnacle,

Its rank guts a fulcrum;

A feast timed
To the tide's pendulum;

Sea-wracked, its rocks
An archive of climate

Locked up like coal.
There are still places

On Earth so remote
They are without shelter.

Their messengers alight
Here, for a moment,

Before the flood's broom.

Northern Wheatear

Here I am, the same colours –
Pit dust on my wing tip,
Radcliffe brick on my breast –

A teaspoon of blood, nerve and feather
Lit for a moment
On the colliery rubble, chipping flint

On a concrete lintel sinking
Into wartime sand. Though I go
By a different name, I am

The same Wheatear you saw
On the dunes that summer
You stepped out of the wet

Scented forest – that swoop
You felt, fear. The same courage.
The same soaring hope.

Tudelum

Who are you? A bone
Flute in your throat,
Nothing but a cry
And a necklace of prints

Lacing wet sand,
A repetitive stitch
In a gansey, a stamp
In funereal clay.

Turnstone, redshank,
Printing the shore
By the Bronze Age cists
At Bondicar,

The storm peels back
A palimpsest,
Tracks in the peat
To the drowned forest.

Sand Martins

If you want to know who we were
Who left our footprints behind us, look no further

Than the mysterious holes in the dune, a few metres
Above its black peat. So quick and alive
Now, and so Other,

All day the sand martins twist and braid, silken
And lethal to the small flies they snap up for their children.

Folded flat, they post themselves into their burrows,
Earth's sweet, damp guts, known only
To those who walk ahead of us. Their squeaks and chirrups

Just as we heard them that summer, a small town
Teeming with families, their little blunt faces

Bursting into the light, until the sky is joyous
With secrets they know and we do not,
Their dark shuttles braiding Now! Now!

Until they are gone.

Bloody Cranesbill

As if it were not purple enough, cranesbill
Argues itself alive, more purple
For its damp, delicious green, more green for its purple –

Magenta, then, against the sward and the elemental
Windswept blue, an argument of pigment,
The Sun's violence firing the factories of its cells,

A contradiction – flimsy-tenacious, its petals
Purple against bird's foot trefoil, the furious yellow ragwort,
A delicate, particular dissonance, harmonic at scale

With skylark and meadow pipit, bloody cranesbill
Splits whiteness into sweetness; then, colouring it visible
For moth and fly and gnat, spins birdsong from sunlight

And, like the hawkbit, borrows a bird's name.

Cormorant

A mad blue startled eye
Stares at the horizon
From the river's mouth.

Dishevelled, a fossil
Has pegged out its oily rags
On the blackened piles.

What am I? Spokes.
A broken umbrella.
A bin-bag. Awkward angles,

A fault in the deep rock.
A long snake gullet,
A guttural squawk:

The clank of rail and staithe.
Shoulders, wings, coal's colours
Trapped in its sheen.

The eye glares. Ice
Thickens. The sea shrinks back
Or swallows a whole forest.

A yolk-yellow billhook
Opens up a place
Of darkness, urgent:

My other self is fluent;
My greed, legendary,
Can swallow a trout whole,

A forest, an ocean
Way out to the horizon.

Cubby

Cubby, ye're a bonny bord. Mild, an' ower-soft,
Wallerin' doon the ooze wi' yer sea-byet feet,
Broon as an' aa'd dopper. Are ye no feart,
Rowellin' aboot the lippers or amang folks?

That much at hyem aboot the wears, ye've disappeart,
Yeer heed's a wadge, yeer neb's a fid, ye sneuk an' plodge
Amang the bents, a heap a barky gear
Bidin' quiet. Wheer's yer man? Awa'.

Ah but in May, daddin' like corky dookas –
Thorty-strang, an' aa' the bonny bairns
Thrustledoon-soft an' sooty, aa't'githor,
Iverybody's business – ye're a hyell village.

Cubby: eider duck, from its association with St Cuthbert; *wallerin':* waddling;
ooze: mud; *sea-byet:* sea-boot; *dopper:* oilskin; *feart:* afraid; *rowellin':* rolling;
lippers: white caps on the sea; *hyem:* home; *wears:* seaweed; *heed:* head;
wadge: wedge; *neb:* beak; *fid:* a spike used to work with rope; *sneuk:* sniff
about; *plodge:* wade; *bents:* coarse sea grass; *barky gear:* fishing gear, tanned
brown with bark; *bidin':* remaining; *daddin':* bobbing; *corky dookas:* cork
floats; *bairns:* children; *thrustledoon:* thistledown; *hyell:* whole.

Birds

Imagine them not here.
No sparrows chattering among the creeves.
No shrieking pickies, swooping down like knives,

The Island stripped of its glitter; no raucous wake
Towed by the trawler fleet; gone, like the corncrake,
The cormorants swept up from the blackened pier.

The sea, rising, breathing, without its benevolent
Company, puffin, eider. The sky empty.
We thought we glimpsed ourselves in them, domestic –

The harrassed blackbird, the monogamous swan.
But the jackdaw's riveted eye was watching us watch it.
If we saw them at all, we sensed in their lightness

Deep time, great distance; every open space,
Back yard and slate roof, hawthorn hedge, horizon,
Connected by them to an immense pulse.

As if the curlew was the cool, damp voice of the river,
And scribbling skylarks summoned the dunes from sleep.
Now over deserted brickyard, boatyard, harbour,

Some ancient music, silently expressed,
Flows and dissolves, made visible by starlings.
Our own inarticulate longings coalesce,

Dissolve and resolve with them. As in a mirror,
Our disembodied feelings find their shape.
Small vessels of imagination – Freedom, flight –

You're hard to separate from who we are
As body is from spirit. When you're gone,
Perhaps you'll leave your calls trapped in our cell-phones,

Pure information, tuned to a secret
Forecast we can't quite hear – tide, season, weather –
Urgent to tell us something. Something important.

creeves: crab and lobster pots; pickies: terns.

44

Fog

Sometimes the world wakes up blind.
That old drone, the foghorn,
Calls you from sleep. The Island,

Harbour, even the street, have vanished. The air
In all its restless, immeasurable complexity –
Invisible rivers, turbulence, vortices,

Bird roads, smelling of sea salt, warm earth, grass –
Rinsed one white. Fog has erased the places
You recognise. The Paddling Pool. The Pier.

The Lighthouse. On the shore the birds are fearless.
They fly almost from underfoot. In the hush
Between the foghorn moans, the edge

Of everything you thought you understood
Presses close, and home
Knows itself, for the first time, by its own voices.

Wishbone

Whose wishbone is this, picked clean
On the North Side, by the boatyard?

Just such a bone
Keeps the world's clock ticking – *tirrick*,

Tarree, teerum, pickie – Arctic tern;
Braces its strong, innumerable upstrokes,

That epic journey back from the cold,
Or whatever becomes of it.

No old boys now by the boatyard to tell the weather
From the crack of the merrythowt

Or the height of a circling gull.
No old wives plotin' whews, afeared to burn feathers.

But the gift shops at the harbour sell silver charms
In the shape of a wishbone,

Which might be the flare
Of a coble's gripe, or the delicate engineering

That kept the allosaurus upright. The North Shore,
Sea-washed and strewn

With bladderwrack, willow-branch, polythene, pebble, bone,
Reminds each one – Be careful

What you wish for.

Linnets

Amble, at your untidy
Edges, where the river has chosen
Its outlet, for now, and the tideline

Endlessly rewrites itself,
A fine cloth shimmers.
How tightly woven

Sunlight, green shoot, grey seed
And these small staccato
Sounds. Another

Summer is over. The linnets
Flit, flash, flicker, thistle to thistle,
Hip to haw, their babble

A small stream's silvery
Brilliance, and whistle
'See you!' 'See you!'

Wishbone *(opposite page)*

tirrick, tarree, teerum, pickie: Northumbrian names for different species of
tern; *merrythowt:* old name for a wishbone; *plotin':* plucking; *whews:* wigeon;
gripe: the wine-glass curve of a coble's bows, which gripped the water.

The Braid

Between the Yacht Club and the Gut, a space
Opens for the imagination. Dog walkers, joggers,
Pushchairs and pensioners – each sees a different place.

To the two women with the bulging carriers, resting tired legs,
The town tip. Childhood's tin cans, blue slag, ashes.
Home, a coal fire at its heart. To their grandkids
Meandering out of school, a big yawn. Grass.

The old man straightens his back, lays down his machine
In what he still calls 'Harrisons'. A white hull floats
In the cradle above his head. He is sanding its keel –
Not a coble's red oak ram, but marine polyethylene.

Behind him rears the new Quay. Smart Scandinavian
Net-loft style apartments dwarf the yard, gaze out
Towards the blue horizon. In the sudden peace,

A silvery, thin sprinkle of glitter. On the Gut
A robin is singing from the fireweed floss;
And half a mile upstream, the Pleistocene
Grey heron shrieks, metallic. Yaws. Takes flight.

Grey Heron

Hunched in his topcoat, tentlike,
He will make himself invisible
For hours, while the river

Gathers together
Sheep stell and salt, where the smolt feel
The sea's pull. Castle, steeple,

Salmon. The Coquet
Broadens. Against a clatter
Of coal staithes, railroads,

Shipyards, his breastbone
A wire coat-hanger,
His cry prehistoric,

He flings the tarpaulin
Of himself a few yards downstream,
Lands in a folding

Of tent-flaps and poles,
Rearranging themselves
In an unexplored country.

The Auld Watter

Flooded, or about to flood,
The saltings stretch between the tides.

Salt, wet, silvery light.
Tree trunks, sand. The wildest place.

Water glitters. Something lets loose
Its cry. A ripple. Rings dilate.

Where once a river emptied out,
Only uncertainty. Over and over

A curlew flings its loop of sound –
Flings it and captures wildness in its noose.

Full Tide on the Coquet

Six o' clock, and home time
On the highway. Headlights.
Quiet illumination –

Sky and river, palest
Lilac, milky. Oyster –
A new moon in the west.

Far off, in the space
Between, a broken necklace
Threads enormous distance,

Scraps from another place –
Frozen, stony – splinters,
Looping closer, arcing

Over the stubble, croaking
Louder in harsh voices,
Scrambled letters – geese –

A fluent line, composing,
Dissolving, rewriting
Imperatives in ancient

Cuneiform. The ice
Is shrinking before us.
But this is sweet September

And the road, a river
In torrent, a spate,
Is urgent to be elsewhere.

Can

On the sand at the Sneuk we found a brittle moon,
Battered, cratered, its edges eaten,
Frosted and scabbed. I think it had fallen

A long way through time from a different planet
Stuck in a groove, beyond recognition,
Altered, like everything round it, in transit.

Off Beadnell Point

If there is a heaven it is here, now, off Beadnell Point.
This road of light.
Dazzle, glitter, shimmer – ceaseless motion
Unrolled to the horizon,
As if a door lay open, and the light spilled out.

You can stare and stare into the sea's cold fire,
Its endless recycling; doing, undoing;
Its setting down its gradual dust – shell, bone –
In new lines; its smoothing
Old, cracked rock with a slow, mechanical roll.

You might hear in its Rush, slosh, a deep roar; ferocious
Immeasurable power.
Enough to sink unconscionable heat,
Lock up the chemistry of spoilt air.
Hush, hush, it murmurs, parental.

You might hear in its Wash, wash, a chance to confess,
Deep absolution. What history calls
Divine fire. You might hear
History endlessly write and rewrite itself, slowly
Erasing its old lines, over and over.

Sandylowper

Not so bad to belong
To the deepest strata,
Or to share with the oldest rock
The colour of its armour,

To burrow in ware-stink
And salty tangle,
Or to sleep in the jewel-box sand
Among its stars and spirals

Millennia. Not so
Terrible, to fuel
The migration of millions, millions,
Thousands of snowy miles,

And, billions strong, become
Silica-crystal, feather;
To store in chitin's curl,
Nerves' flex and flick, the future.

A shock, then, that each one
Wants not to die,
Popping like corn in a skillet
Ahead of this hissing tide.

Sandylowper: sand-hopper; *ware:* seaweed.

A Lang Way Hyem

What is this blue line stretching away?
High dunes, wide sky,
Cold inrush of salt. Will it never be still?

Is it coble and net? A lugworm knot?
Is it bucket and spade?
Footprints, large, small, erased by the tide?

Bladderwrack crackling under a boot?
Whose tale does it tell?

FIRST RESIDENT
This village has changed so much. My father used to
say there were only 50 houses here before the War.
But every village is the same along the coast now.
More tourism. The businesses couldn't cope without
the tourism. But that's progress!

CONSERVATION OFFICER
The biggest issue in this village is second home ownership.
Holiday homes. It's the highest in the country now. More
than half second or holiday homes. You've got to question
the sustainability of the community.

While rooftops and building sites hunker inland
Does it unwind for miles in the hand over hand

Of a fisherman's line? *Is it marram grass*
Combed in the wind?

As the Sun spills its silver
Out across Beadnell Bay,

Rolling deep cloud-shadows over the dunes
From Featherblaa' south to the Long Nanny Burn
And the scoop of the shore down to Newton, one sheer flow –

Has a gull, in one sweep of its effortless wingtip, drawn it?

BIRD WARDEN

You don't need a bird book any more. You can use an app.
We've got swallows going past, sand martins, they're nesting
behind the limekilns. You can see the Long Nanny Burn
from here, the river. We have special birds that come back
every year to nest there. Little terns, that have come
from Africa, and Arctic terns that come from Antarctica.

HOLIDAY FAMILY

We come every year for our holidays. My son's nine now.
For him to come to the coast, get off his gadgets, turn
the wi-fi off, is a welcome relief for us all.

BIRD WARDEN

The little terns only like to nest in a very particular
area, that sand-spit at the Long Nanny. We feel a
responsibility to help these birds. We want to make it
sustainable, before they become extinct, like the dodo.

Silent. A sail-boat glides over the bay's glitter.
Clink-clink-clink, halyards on metal masts
Chatter at the tide's edge, whisper of departure.

FIRST RESIDENT

In my grandfather's day they fished for herring and cod and
haddock and plaice. But it ended up with just the crabs and lobsters,
and the salmon fishing in the summer. The nets are out now. See
the pink buoys and white corks at the Cundy? That's a salmon berth.
There's Featherblaa', Behind the Carrs, the Pier Stones. The Long
Nanny's the Burn. He's got the nets shot there. This is a scene that
really hasn't changed, not for hundreds and hundreds of years.

Hardest to see what is really here.

A tern-haunted beach. A swallow-swooped harbour.
High stone limekilns: a hollow shell, empty of labour.
Rooted between them, this serpent-headed bench;

And fringing its bank-top, white-crowned plantains
Shiver and nod, while the feathery grasses
Shake in the wind till the pollen scatters.

SECOND RESIDENT
*I get quite surprised when I drive through other
villages and I see children waiting for buses or walking
down the street. They're an endangered species in this
village. There are very few people left in the village who
were born here. In a way, we've been hollowed out.*

The sea has thrown up fistfuls of knives,
Paper-cuts, screams, a blizzard of five-pointed stars.
Will they never rest?

Terns – each fork-tailed, feather and bone,
Delicate as insects,
Almost weightless, white as the Moon.

How far have they travelled?
Antarctic ice in their streamlined angles,
Sand-eel metal, and another element –

Flickering reptilian ratchet and screech,
Prehistoric
Sandpaper shrieks, exigent, endlessly multiple –

The voice of the sand-spit before speech.

*Bad luck, stick your thumbs up,
Better touch caa'd iron –
Iv'rybody i' the syem boat, hinny –
Saa't on the fire!*

57

The little terns are a number one protected bird. They're the
dodo. If we don't do anything about it, it will be the end.

Out at the Long Nanny Burn, the river writhes.
Hefts tonnes, grain by grain, rewrites itself overnight;

Flattens its small mesas, drives its crumbling canyons,
Telescopes millennia into a tide or two.

BIRD WARDEN

So we've got a North wind. The birds are sitting with their
beaks into the wind, hunkering down, keeping warm.

Here on the beach, the ice-fields have only just retreated.
The headlands that anchor it, older still – prehuman,
Every day, twice a day, created from new:

Sediments of a world remaking itself. Creatures
Buried in darkness for billions of sunsets,
Washed into daylight, shifting, impermanent –

A deep, slow undertow; a surface glitter.
Time, and the Long Nanny's currents
Grinding against one another.

FIRST FISHERMAN

I've been fishing 40 years, I think. That's my boat,
'The Supreme'. It's a Northumberland coble. Grand
sea boats, yes. There's not many left. They're gonna
be a thing of the past, cobles. The yards that used to
build them, they're all gone. It's a craft that's handed
down, see. They're built by the eye. There's never two
alike. Aye, it's a shame that there's gonna be none left.

Slime, drip, pop. A musky, genital stink,
Slithery crevices, leathery forests,

Numberless limpets, buckies, whullicks
Grazing the sandstone plains, their barnacle cities'

White encrustation, clinging on.
Claws, pincers, snapping jaws; wildest, most violent

Factory, turning the sea's imperceptible sparks –
Plants, animals, countless rivers of stars

Tinier than a sand grain, a dust mote –
Into something sharper than teeth. Pure appetite;

As if the rocks themselves – the Sneuk, the Carrs –
Were nothing but a hunger
To be elsewhere, and other.

FIRST FISHERMAN

I've fished about seven mile off in that, which is a lang way.
You've got to have one eye on the weather and one eye on
what you're doin'. If the weather breaks, it's a lang way
to come hyem.

FIRST RESIDENT

O the superstitions! You couldn't say the word for the animal
with the curly tail. P-I-G. (Sorry! Put your thumbs up.) They
wouldn't launch their boat if it was just painted on a Friday –
bad luck. If it hadn't been a good catch Uncle Charlie used
to take a handful of salt and throw it into the fire.

Here comes *The Supreme*, steaming into harbour
With a box of blue-black lobsters, snapping, gleaming fossils
Hauled up alive out of the Cretaceous forest
Sixty-million years ago, and twenty fathoms deep.

Cork rope, quoit rope, salmon net an' anchor,
Featherblaa', the Cundy, Back a the Carrs,
Keep an eye on the weather, it's a lang road hyem –
Saa't on the fire!

59

The Arctic terns land on the sand-spit and get the desirable
residences above the high water. The little terns are smaller.
They're bullied down to the edge of the sand-spit by the bigger
birds. So what we have to do is intervene and help them.
If we didn't intervene the eggs would just be washed out to sea.

CONSERVATION OFFICER
This is my work patch. I look after this coast. It's an Area of
Outstanding Natural Beauty. My job is to make sure that its
natural beauty is there for future generations to enjoy. To conserve
and enhance. It's not always easy to get the balance right.

Honk, squeal, bubble, rattle and shriek:
Prehuman syllables float from the Burn –
Rivers of voices flood in and drain out again.

Sift and scatter. The Long Nanny
Haps up and buries. Bird bone. Memory.
Spring tides of strange tongues, settlements slipping –

Brunton Burn, blunt Anglo-Saxon, the glint of an ancient
Coin, never displaced by the new word, 'River'.
Nanny. *Nanny*: a deeper history of water

Repeatedly stripped clean in the endless argument –
Fresh, salt, wrangling; churning its sediments.

FISHERIES SCIENTIST
Salmon and sea trout come back after anything from one year
to three years. At the moment we think only about 5 or 6%
of salmon that go into the sea come back as adults. Fifteen or
or twenty years ago we believe that number was closer to 10%.
Survival at sea appears to be reducing.

I remember watching the boats come in, the men hauling up the boxes
of crabs and lobsters. Then they would get into the salmon boats
and go and shoot the nets. It was long days for them, but
it was in their blood. They loved it.

FISHERIES SCIENTIST

Some of these salmon will head off to the Norwegian Sea, some
will head off to the Faroes and Greenland. We think that when
they smolt and leave a river, they imprint with the chemical
nature of that river. They can almost smell the river, so when
they come back as adults, they can sense which river is theirs.

Twist, splice, snip. Four sharp little pairs of scissors;
Four needles, four shuttles,
Knitting invisible streamers in and out the harbour.

Swallows. Blue-black mechanical
Traps, sprung from the insects
That fuel their long haul,

Iron-oxide and rust, magnetised
To and away from each other, skimming the pier,
The deserted limekilns – far and near,

Here and gone, deft, swift, their familiar
Clamour a sheer voice of summer.

And in the deep stillness of evening, at the Burn,
Up from the saltmarsh and abandoned farm,
Petrol blue, they speed, glide and fold themselves

Under the footbridge, exact
As a pin-prick in a map,

Though their Beadnell-hatched young have not yet
Tasted the earthy African sunlight and heat.
What's Home? A secret

Repeating itself – a precise
Pendulum tick, a heartbeat –
Ebb, and flow, and breath, and tide, and season.

YOUNG FISHERMAN

I've been out in the boat with Dad since 6 o' clock this mornin'.
Dad can't pass the licence on to me, no. It's not hereditary any more.

In the Arctic sway of the Greenland Sea,
The salmon remembers with its whole body.

YOUNG FISHERMAN

When I was a kid, when I was in school, in the summer holidays,
I always was on the boat with Granddad. I've always done it.

Slowly, it feels its way along roads of unknowing,
In strands of varying salinity, tasting its path,
Swilling the bitter salt through its feathery gills;

YOUNG FISHERMAN

Dad an' Granddad's taught us everything I know about it.

The tug of a magnet, a chemical imprint, remembered
River fug of gravel and mud, exact as a sat-nav.
Where is it heading? To the end of its longing.

YOUNG FISHERMAN

One of the biggest fish I ever caught was with
Granddad, just behind the harbour. There's a picture in
the house of Granddad, the fish an' me. The fish from
tail to head is standin' taller than us. I think it was a
22 pound salmon, it was. Aye, it was bigger than me!

Cork rope, quoit rope, salmon net an' anchor,
Featherblaa', the Cundy, Back a the Carrs,
Keep an eye on the weather, it's a lang road hyem –
Saa't on the fire!

FISHERIES SCIENTIST

What's happened is a thing called the Net Limitation Order.
Once the licence runs out, it can't be passed on, because of the
worries about the levels of stocks of salmon. It's sensitive, obviously.
It's people's livelihood. The last thing anyone wants to do is prevent
someone from carrying on with their livelihood. But we have
to look at the status of the salmon stocks, and we have to make
sure that that stock is protected into the future. Difficult decisions
have to be made to ensure the long-term survival of the species.

Thrash, thump, slap. A shower of sequins –
Scales, salt droplets, and the fresh stink of fish,
Metallic, silvery – ocean's weight and distance,
Heft, muscle, its gleaming quick element
Come to rest beside a black rubber boot.

Bad luck, stick your thumbs up,
Better touch caa'd iron –
Iv'rybody i' the syem boat, hinny –
Saa't on the fire!

FIRST RESIDENT

They made all their own crab pots out of hazel. They used to bend
the hazel and put it in the base. Knit all the nets that went over
the top. They had what they called 'netting needles' – they were a
long needle, a foot long almost, and they used to knit the covers.

Quick as a needle, a swallow sweeps the strand-line.

Knuckles of oar weed, rubbery bladderwrack
Ravelled with fishing twine, crab shells, a crackle of plastic.

Displaced, reassembled: kelp stipe and creeve bow, blue tubing
Colonised, barnacled, scribbled with sea lace,

White polystyrene eroding to oolites,
To snow-thaw, the creak of an ice sheet, snapping, collapsing.

The seaweed's breaking down, it's feeding the micro-organisms,
it's giving food to the birds, because the birds are going
to eat the bugs; there's a whole food chain that needs the
seaweed to break down. So it might smell horrible and I
might walk past quick, but it's important – it's all part
of the ecology of the site. It's a big circle.

A mile from the terns' prehistoric racket,
A salmon flips. The lazy sail-boat ratches,

And on the high wave-crests of dunes, wind sings in the grasses.
What each knows of time or place is only its parish.

TWO TEENAGE BOYS ON HOLIDAY

I think it might be a place to be when we're older.

My Mum wants to stay here when she's retired.

We'll come back with our own boys…

… Hopefully…

…Hopefully. If we find anyone…

Yeah. If we find anyone.

Every time we come down here, we picture Granddad –
the things we did with him.

We're kind of celebrating his life with us.

A whullick, a sand-eel, a sand-hopper, something smaller
Wriggling in the kelp forests, foraging, feeding the silver
Smolt in a delicate mesh of air and water.

Splash! A fish. Its shining rings dilate,
Dissolving, disappearing, spreading out and out.

Intricately ravelled in its net of light,
Minutely local creatures, intimate,

Entangled here, now, every ripple travelling
From the hottest desert, to the polar ice,
From a time before speech to time after counting.

SECOND RESIDENT

I don't think that there really is a tension with tourism here.
No, not at all. We don't want to lose the tourism, we need it.
We welcome people. We love seeing new people every week.
It's just when it tips over into the majority of houses being
holiday houses and second homes, then that affects the sustainability
of the community. There needs to be some sort of halt, and more
of a community living here, with the tourism weaving in and out.

Ribbed sky, ridged sand. The beach dazzles,
Reinventing itself with every tide.

Across the snake-headed bench, exquisitely patient,
A spider grapples its strand. A swallow glides,

Skimming the harbour, empty of cobles;
Scoops the puddled mud from a building site.

BIRD WARDEN

Nature's the best. It's sharing with me. It's letting me
find an orchid that's just coming up. If I rush past at
100 miles an hour, I'm not going to see that orchid.
I've got to help nature share with us, so that it can
keep growing and so that we're conserving it and
sharing it with everybody, so that when I'm not here
the orchids are still here and the little terns are still
here, and everybody enjoys it as much as they do now.

SECOND RESIDENT

Every time there's a high tide, the shape of the Long
Nanny changes. If you go along in a week's time it'll
be a different shape. The river will have changed course.
Where there's sand flats at the moment you won't be able to
get round. Then go in another week and it's wide open again.
It's ever-changing. Maybe the village is like that, too.

Hardest to see what is really here.

Gobbling the green fields, 'Holiday Developments' –
Bellowing dinosaurs ripping up the delicate
Invisible threads.

Now switch off your screen-time,
Quiet the wi-fi, your smartphone, the cliché,
The monotone money talks. What is this endless

Shimmering filigree stretching away?

WHISPER

In a car park on the tarmac,
In a hard hat on a worksite,
In a fast train going nowhere,
In a high rise, in a heartbeat,
In a live feed on a headset,
In a download from a website,
We are balancing the outcome,
We are managing the impact –
The survival of the species;
We are dreaming
The fresh of the tide
And the white wings' lift-off and shriek
And the stink of the seaweed.

Bad luck, stick your thumbs up,
Better touch caa'd iron –
It's a lang road hyem an' ye
Canna torn the clock back –
Saa't on the fire!

Cork rope, quoit rope,
Salmon net an' anchor,
Featherblaa', the Cundy,
Back a the Carrs,
Iv'rybody i' the syem boat, hinny –

Saa't on the fire!

Hyem: home; *caa'd:* cold; *syem:* same; *saa't:* salt; *buckies:* whelks; *whullicks:* winkles; *quoit rope:* sole rope of salmon net, weighted with metal quoits; *the Cundy:* name of one of the salmon-netting berths in Beadnell Bay. A *cundy* is a drain; *creeve:* crab or lobster pot; *ratches:* tacks; *smolt:* a young salmon before it leaves the river.

Goldcrests

First sign, the faintest sound –
Invisible needlepoint tattoos the garden.
Whisked in on a south-east gale, fairy-lights

Twinkle in the apple boughs,
Dapple and vanish, becoming leaves,
Becoming shadow. Where

Have they birled in from, this windfall
Bundle of contradictions, shy, hidden?
Black beetle eyes, thorn-stab, but round

And soft as plums, crowned brilliant
Ochre, as if each skull was split
Open, as Earth is, by its own fire.

A flicker on the margin, their flight
And pin-prick calls' starlight glitters
Across day's drab garden, bringing

Wildness, and when they're gone –
Off in a whirl of blown leaves – the apple trees
Stand, for the first time, bare.

Arguments

Not *too much swell* but *ower-much sea*;
Not *a choppy day* but *a lipper on the wetter* –

A hobble, a wabble, a bit top rabble;
Then *a wund for' the eastard, the seas mekkin'*;

Rowelley. Gurrelly. Nowt but smoke –
In the thick of the spindrift *ye darsent look.*
Ye knew where y' wore b' the sea's brek.

Seven old fishermen in a smoky hut.
Seven points of view. Relentless arguments,

Almost inaudible. Hush. The sea's susurration.
Countless lost salt tongues. Ceaseless translation.

lipper: short, choppy seas; *hobble, wabble, top rabble:* a surface roll; *rowelly:* bigger seas; *gurrelly:* wild, stormy seas; *smoke:* spindrift; *brek:* break.

The Long Line

When Thomas Skee
First cranked the handle
And the *Golden Horn*

Spluttered into smoky life,
And a flock of dunlin
Scattered from the Haven,

He had no idea what he had started.

From the sea, the landmarks –
Langstone, the Crumstone,

Staggart, the Castle – looked
The same. Inland,
Wattie's horse

Tugged at the heck,
And at the Square Bill Liddell's
Cuddy trembled.

Too far to see
With any telescope
From the coppiced hazel stick

To the thousand stacked black creeves
Of steel and plastic;
Too far to measure

From the coble's graceful figure eight,
Long ratch and flight,
Creature of wind and water,

To the slick pair-trawlers' smash-and-grab,
Pillage by sonar, radar,
Colour plotter.

Aa'd Skee and Hannah
Knew the wind
But not what made it blow.

You can be o'er-sharp,
Or, if not o'er-sharp,
O'er-slow.

WHISPER
I' the dark a the morn' wi' pokes an' sacks,
Bend t' the musshels, creels cuttin' wor backs,
Heft 'em hyem t' the cracket t' skeeyn,
Finn'gers fleein' like a sharp machine –
Dabs 'n' sprags 'n' git muckle haddocks
Fr' the Two Hoor Grund…

It was you, Jane Douglas,
Bella, Meggie, Kate,

Skeeyning the sweet
Salt orange gristle,
Bait neat as knitting,

While your men become one
With the boat – a beast
Of many legs, half-human

Sea-worm, slipping between
This world and another:
T'gither noo: Howway, HOOP!

Their dark tide rises, gathers –
Charlie, Teedle, Stephen –
Heaves and falls away.

Sharp gripe, bite the grease.
A coble is history.
It carries a whole village –

Sing her down to the sea.

Heuks for' the Square t' the Steed an' Benty.
Fowerteen-hunnert's mair n' plenty.
Varnigh slavery. Aa' for family.
Canna mek a better on it. Jiggered at thorty.

Where are you now, Tom Skee,
Hannah, Mary Anne?
The lipper's needle, shuttle,

Knitting your mortal
Twine to its shining mash.
The tide is going out.

On the bank top
A black hut, abandoned.
Long bents hush over the bark pots.

Older than writing, their skills –
Heuk, sneeyd, swull;
Their seamark maps, old wives' tales,

Invisible constructions
Grander than castle walls.

Unpick the mash. Unhitch the knot,
An' heuk bi heuk we'll lowse 'em oot.
The haddock, the keek, the sprag, the pout...

Haul down your halyard. Haul,
Fawcus, Douglas, Dixon,
Till the tanned sail fills,

Liddell, Ste'en, Hall.
Pick up your graithing-iron,
Hundyside, Murkwell.

Aa' the aa'd'ns, listen:
The Braille of the ground
You grappled hand over hand –

Crumstone inside a Langstone,
Hebron on Featherblaa' –
Encodes its hard lesson.

Farewell to the red sail
Dipping under the horizon.

Our beautiful machines
Have severed the long line.

The school of wind and water
Leaves nothing behind.

Long Line: traditional winter fishing gear carrying 1,400 hooks, each of which needed to be baited daily with mussels. This unpaid work was usually done by women; *heck:* hay rack; *cuddy:* donkey; *creeve:* lobster or crab pot; *ratch:* tack; *poke:* bag; *cracket:* stool; *skeeyn:* shell mussels and limpets as bait for long lines; *dabs:* sole; *sprags:* large codling; *Howway, HOOP!:* chant of men launching the coble; *gripe:* the sharp flare of a coble's bow, by which it gripped the water; *jiggered:* worn out; *lipper:* short, white-topped waves; *bents:* sea grass; *heuk, sneeyd, swull:* hook, snood and basket for the long lines. A sneeyd or snood connected each hook to the line; *keek:* a type of haddock; *pout:* a type of whiting; *lowse:* loosen; *graithing-iron:* grappling-iron.

A Hut a Byens

Skyeldeman, wor nyems, fetched far fr' hyem,
Hanted amang ee, a hut a byens
Happed up wi' sand ahint the Fairen.

Hunkered i' the Boolie Hyel,
Waitin' on a hooley
T' howk 'em oot, th' baad unkent. The shaed

Craa'd roond the tide clock. Fr' the dockens
A styenchat chittered.
Wund arselled, an' the sea myed.

Byens, claed wi' bents, unbegretten; words
Graithed fr' the far deeps; sneeyds
Berrelled t'gither i' the sea's roads.

Skeyney's Carr, Glororum, the Skaithe, the Gwat,
Bebbla-Wingate, Peb the Nack.
Th' rattle roond yor mooth like styens –

Aa'd Cubby's beads –
Thoo the soond a yor gran' bairns'
Greet-gran' bairns setten 'em doon

Maa'n be theor last faerin'.

hut: heap; *byens:* bones; *Skyeldeman:* name used on Holy Island for people
from Seahouses on the mainland, and elsewhere to mean 'stranger'; *nyems:*
names; *hyem:* home; *hanted:* hung around; *happed:* covered; *ahint:* behind, in
the lee of; *the Fairen:* Inner Farne; *hunkered:* crouched; *Boolie Hyel:* the Bowl
Hole; *hooley:* storm; *howk:* dig, unearth; *baad:* remained (p.p. of bide);
unkent: unknown; *shaed:* shade; *craa'd:* crawled; *tide clock:* a carved stone
used to tell the time of Mass. There is one in the wall of St Aidan's Church

crypt, Bamburgh; *dockens:* dock leaves; *styenchat:* stonechat; *arselled:* backed; *myed:* made, grew; *claed:* clothed; *bents:* coarse dune grass; *unbegretten:* unmourned; *graithed:* grappled; *sneeyds:* snoods, thin twine connecting hooks to fishing lines; *berrelled:* spun; *Skeyney's Carr, Glororum, the Skaithe, the Gwat, Bebbla-Wingate, Peb the Nack:* local place names and navigation marks; *styens:* stones; *Cubby's beads:* fossil crinoids, known locally as 'St Cuthbert's beads'; *maa'n:* may; *faerin':* journey.

The Tide Clock

From St Aidan's a blackbird
Calls into the dark
At Matins – a gleam
In a bowlful of stars.

At Prime, the irascible
Wren, Jenny Bell,
Scolds from the brambles
Around Hannah's Well.

At Terce, the hinds' children,
Skipping to school
Down the Wynding, play chase
With the wittery-wagtail.

At Sext, seeking gulls' eggs,
Five fishers of Farne
Hear the amorous Cuddy ducks'
Wooing. At None

On Spindlestone Heugh,
A peasweep storm –
A sky-serpent, writhing.
The tractor turns home,

And at Vespers the spuggy
Flies into the lit
Hall of the Castle –
Becomes permanent.

Then over the Bowl Hole
A robin will keep
The evening's last offices,
Darker than sleep.

Jenny Bell: a local name for the wren; *Hannah's Well:* well at the foot of
Bamburgh Castle; *hinds:* agricultural labourers; *the Wynding:* a lane in
Bamburgh; *wittery-wagtail:* pied wagtail; *Cuddy ducks:* eider ducks, named
after St Cuthbert; *Spindlestone Heugh:* a rocky outcrop associated with an
ancient Wyrm legend; *peasweep:* lapwing; *spuggy:* sparrow, as in St Bede's
'Ecclesiastical History'; *The Bowl Hole:* a hollow in the dunes beneath
Bamburgh Castle containing an Anglo-Saxon cemetery.

The Fulmar

I watch the fulmar hurl his breast
To the wind's unseen geometry;
Spread wings on nothing, reckless of gravity,
And ride that risk
And rest
On sheer uncertainty

Choosing no choice.

I must learn to be like him,
To follow the reach and search of air –
Swoop, sink, stand, balance, soar on the invisible spiral stair –
And not resist
But trust,
And be carried there.

The Old Lifeboat House

What are we doing here,
Scrubbing cobwebs from the eyes of the old lifeboat house
In the dazzle out to Hobthrush?

These are not our
Sons, neighbours, torn from field or firelight
In Fiddler's Green or Marygate by the crack of a gun.

I did not drown my sorrows for the woman running
Helter-skelter down Lewins Lane in her shawl and pinny.

Have we no history of our own to polish?

The wind blows an eddy of dust over the neat flagstones.
The lifeboat house with its new roof
Has a hollow sound, empty, like England,

Perched on a bleak shore, sparkling and half-abandoned,
Jingling a few coins in its pocket,
Waiting for its volunteers;

For the sea-worm with many legs
That heaves itself over green mountains – heaves
Hearts into the mouths of a whole village –

And down the street
Old men with voices like shovels full of cinders,
Women with knuckles cracked like brown loaves,

Come running, running, running, their hearts on fire.

Many Hands

Prins Knud, 1940

Then every adult man
And shawl-happed, creel-huddled woman – a great crowd –
Sea-boot to spade lug, began

Howking a channel in the February sleet.
Higher than the herring house, the length of Fenkle Street:
Three smoky tug-boats had failed to shift her. Together,

Ungrudging, a ragged patchwork, they bowed,
Strained, buckled down, volunteered themselves. They were a team –
A crew, an unruly chorus, a congregation

Rattling the rafters. A family; the perfect engine,
Heads bent on salvage, backs to the weather,
In the shadow of that iron hulk, some of them remembered

Mothers, fathers, who could move mountains.

happed: wrapped; *howking:* digging.

Gleaners

Emanuel Head has forgotten the flocks of barked sails
Chasing a china-blue horizon; Steel End, its rookery –

Kipper-smoke, cooper, curses, peaked cap and gansey,
Laughter at the Popple Well, hobnail on cobble, Scotch gutters
Linking arms down Marygate as they knit themselves into history.

Sea-smack in a hollow rock, bright efflorescence of rust,
Dressings of yellow trefoil: Ness End has forgotten the clatter –

Clang, shouts, hooves on the polished rails, dust,
Smoke and a sunset-flare from the kiln down at Kennedy.

Wind in the long grass, wave after wave, you have forgotten
Tettie shaa', water butt, box-bed, blackened grate,
Kale raa', hen cree, guffy and netty. Who are these gleaners

Without root or anchor, picking up buttons and pieces
Of blue and white playgen by the path to the glittering Slakes?

barked: steeped in tannin-rich bark; *cooper:* overseer of herring yard, who made barrels; *gansey:* fisherman's jersey, knitted by womenfolk; *gutters:* lasses who travelled down the coast gutting and packing herring; *tettie shaa':* potato plant; *box-bed:* wooden cupboard bed, a protection in poor, damp, draughty cottages; *kale raa':* row of kale or cabbage; *cree:* coop; *guffy:* pig; *netty:* outside lavatory; *playgen:* scraps of broken pottery.

Philadelphia

Something has gone out of this place. Some fiery magic.

Between the East Coast Mainline and the German Ocean
Silence at Pancheek, at Sandbanks

Wide sky and emptiness.

A structure full of its own darkness
Sings in the wind like a strange drum.

And me in my motorcar, I'm speeding across the causeway,
Over the sea-pink distance from wherever I began,

Into this new place, hooked by its brilliance,
To weave myself thread by thread into an old fabric.

Gateway

You've come here 'to get away from it all'; meaning what, exactly?
To lose yourself in this place,
Immersed in the Island's cleansing light, amid the stones' austerities.
You have come for its old promise, peace.

But it splinters – glints, braids, knots with the tide streams. Day trippers,
Locked in their desire-lines, flow and eddy, and the swallows fly
Their blue-black criss-cross loop and lace back again, swooping
Through the Priory's ruined eye

To the grim block set against the Scots; while under the brae,
At the keel's wet edge, in a shiver of shale and ore,
A red-bearded quarryman innocently wipes his hands
Of distant engines, unspecific wars.

Red List Species

Dianthus deltoides

Small, a fallen star
Snipped out by pinking shears
Among the lemon trefoils,

Its candyfloss colour
Holding a crimson target
For bees, thrives

Here, by a sequence of accidents.
By the exact grace
Of cold quartz dolerite.

By permission of the absolute black
That tucks up
Its astonishing first-born.

By the needle's eye, the Island.
By the miracle of the window
That tots up its pittance of light:

The thin pink five-petalled flower
Hoards its mite of pollen
Between the field of headstones

And the road to the lifeboat house,
One in a starry lonnen, here
Because it can be.

Absences

A drystone wall down the Straight Lonnen –
Lilburn, Cromarty, Selby, Luke and Henderson –
Flowers with yellow crottle, fritillaries, hawthorn.

Out there, the grey sea, many fathoms –
Fenham Granary ower Beal Muck Midden.
Wilson, Allison, Brigham, Patterson, Shell.

A spade strikes brick brash, a clay pipe, pan-tile.
Drysdale, Douglas, Allan, Kyle and Markwell.
Gnarled hands hold out an empty kale-pot,

Eloquent as absence. *Bebbla-Wingate.*
Spider-threads, invisible, blown on the west wind.
The stones hold together, nothing between them.

Woven

Fisherwoman of the fields, her net
Heavy with gnats,
Tow stretched taut to its tense grass kedge,

A spider has woven the sticky basket of her nest
Under the criss-cross willow sculpture
At the gate from the Lonnen to the sea of dunes.

Standing guard by the egg sac as the hours
Tilt towards winter, the work of her eight fingers
Replicated ceaselessly, a clenched fist,

She bides, deceitful; yarn-spinner, spider
Bearing the white image of the grass flower
On her green back. She belongs to the grass

And the grass to her, and the whole wide Island.

Beblowe

Quaking Grass, Soft Brome, Squirrel-tail Fescue
Flower without name. What am I? No one.

Invisible pollen-sweet waves sweeping into the future,
Over and through them, a knotwork: earthworm, lark song.

Kelp-burner, braider of creels, Irish hands, drystone-waller,
Stitching yourself into the Island's irregular weave –

Lime-slaker, kale-stirrer, gooseberry-picker, bait-skeeyner,
Dislocated blow-in, carrying wristwatch and camera –

Inventing yourself as you go, multiple, syncretic,
Dropping your stitch and picking it up, you will know

Warp and woof when you find it, you will feel
Familial shelter.

kale: broth; *skeeyner:* one who shells mussels for bait, usually women.

Anonymous

Spray-paint on the concrete gun emplacement.
Where does it come from, this urge to decorate?
Galloping straight from the cave wall, so deep

That light cannot reach it. The effigy's magic.
The Instagram to say, I was here. But here, where the gulls
Settle and lift, to stumble across four

Willow-woven brent geese, caught in mid-flight
Near the hide at the Lough's edge, and know
Nothing about their maker,

Seems entirely right: as if
They have risen straight from water and soil
Where they have lain for thousands of years, like the lost skill

Of naming something precisely, without words.

Dig

Blackbird, tail up on the spoil-heap,
Eye pinned to the spade's bite –

Crumbs of soil
Clinging to his whiskers and his yellow trowel –
Flitting so lightly, no one has noticed him.

All week the shadows
Bend to the dull weight of flagstones,
An empty bucket, a wheelbarrow.

These hands – what have they done
But raise crude walls in the June drizzle?
Lose and uncover them again

In the time it takes a cock bird
To dart between the austere stone
War memorial and the black beacon.

Hands, minds, spade, chisel, hammer,
Bible and iPhone, grappling with Eternity. All week
They have heaped up rubble, and questions:

All their scribes, all their illuminations,
All the scholars of Europe and Palestine,
Seoul, Cupertino or England, cannot explain

This – in the quiet light
At dawn or the day's end, a blackbird
Opens his beak

And fourteen hundred summers are one summer.

Arctic Terns

How far they have travelled.
Farther than the pilgrim
Worrying a crinoid rosary.

Farther than the blue-eyed sailor,
A tarred rope in one fist,
In the other, a knife.

Farther than papyrus
From smashed pillar,
Scorched ochre; farther

Than any of these, they have come,
A glittering ice-storm
From the frayed ends of the Earth.

Their clockwork din the racket
Of endless summer,
Their wings' white nights, the Sun

And Moon's altercation,
Their hollow bones inscribing
Pages of skeer and carr,

Strangers all, they alight
Here, on the North Shore,
Knowing what we cannot –

To answer as one flock,
Floating between its farthest
Past and remotest future

Where the bent-grass root
Binds, for a time,
The thing in flight –

Even the grass, xylem and water,
Chlorophyll, light.

Begin Again

Out on the Slakes between two tides, a fresh start
Opens before you – cold, rippled, salt
All the way to the steely breakers. One long thought:

How astonishing to be alive. To walk together
On the worm-knotted sand, light scudding over it, some
Pleistocene colony howling distantly,

A blue bead in an inky ocean. Astonishing to know it,
Telescoped into the hollow of your skull, light
Sizzling starry between the synapses, and at your feet

Countless splintered mirrors, glittering. You're suddenly glad
Of tea-cups, hands, companionable laughter,
The Sun breaking through, your friendships' watch and compass –

Your prints disappearing in the amnesiac mud, as if
None of it mattered as much as you thought it did.

Cocklawburn

Kids from Scremerston
Hang out in the dunes with bottles.
Somebody's children

Have been here a long time,
Rearranging the archive. Playful
Gods, so old they have forgotten

Their names, making themselves visible,
Mixing themselves different
Each time, a new gadget:

Star, whorl, ladder, spiral,
Stuttering, repeating itself, never
The same – a handful

Of sand. Coral, pink flower, relic animal
Pretending to be rock, fossil –
Photo in mineral.

Yes, this is Cocklawburn, pick-axed, coal-nibbled,
Carbon black, furnace-fired, flipped
On its head. At night you can feel

Some current drag you, while the stars
Glint, innumerable
As sand grains, with the whole

Machine on shuffle.

#rhizodont

Then, in a flash,
It claps shut – an ambush –
Teeth, fangs, tusks – crunch, rip,

Snap. The rhizodont,
Dragging itself out of water.
The old world sinks and slips

Beneath its tilted strata.
We're all on a journey.
This one's about us

Unearthing ourselves from a place –
Somatic, interlaced –
To be conjured from light, and sent

Invisible, everywhere,
For everyone to possess.
The children stare at their phones,

A fervent, lit up,
Incorporeal congregation,
Some deep, residual

Root in a life everlasting
Outlasting them, like a fossil
Sarcopterygian fish.

BOOK II

INVISIBLE EVERYWHERE

Organic

A slow snow is drifting

Down, down, to settle
In the speechless dark.
Limestone. Chalk.

Coccolith, coralline.
The sea is dreaming
In its chemical sleep,

Fantastical shapes
With every breath,
Whorl, star, hexagon, spiral,

Locking and unlocking,
Shell, skeleton, pearl;
Crab and coral and whelk.

Do not walk to its edge to seek
Meaning. You will hear
Only dissolution,

Precipitation. Sparkle
And glitter; wave
After wave – hiss –

In conversation with air
Its factories' immense
Chemical reservoirs sizzle.

Sea Chant 2 (opposite page)
tide's brek: point at which the tide turns; *mekkin':* growing; *ootrogue:* rip tide;
lipper: white caps.

Sea Chant 1

Pebble rattle
Rock clatter
Shingle clink and
Cobble racket

Rake-pebble
Stone babble
Round-rolled
Rock rabble

Sea lather
Spume sizzle
Bubble crackle
Surf fizz

Spindrift
Salt spit
Fresh froth
Foam hiss.

Sea Chant 2

A strong breeze, a gentle breeze, a light air, a calm,
A moderate gale, a fresh gale, a whole gale. A storm.

Not the suck back but the tide's brek;
Not a wind from the East but the seas mekkin';
Not the spindrift but the sea-smoke;
Not a clock-calm morn but an ootrogue.

Not too much swell but ower-much sea;
Not a choppy day but a lipper on the wetter.
A strong breeze, a gentle breeze, a light air, a calm,
A moderate gale, a fresh gale, a whole gale. A storm.

The Website at the End of the World

To the Museum of the Future I bequeath
My digital footprint;
My wandering snail-trail of websites, my cookies, my clickbait,
My peculiar archived obsessions, orientations,
My status updates, my step-count, my heart-rate, my Fitbit,
My jumbled cupboards, the dreams that I do not remember,
What I did, what I said, where I went in my head, and with whom.
What I actually probably thought when I thought I thought different.

When I Googled my future – my Final Judgement
A boot-sale of data, my immortal soul
A shimmering hologram of preferences, proclivities – my shame,
The banal inside-out of my Favourites, was indexed, on show.
It predicted the loop of my contacts, faces at my funeral –
Their marks out of ten, unacceptable opinions,
Personal anxieties, body mass index, their probable death-dates.
Your name.

Your phone wants to guess the end of this poem
Based on the premise that you demand more of the same.

INGENIOUS

1 Autonomous

I

Imagine you have a third eye.
Where will you place it?

Imagine a sense that allows you to suddenly
See in the dark.

Imagine your eyes could unscramble the spectrum
Beyond the peep-hole of their own prison.

Think of your fingers making a fist,
Locking around your phone, its screen;
A stone-age axe at the end of your wrist.

> *The world is moving in its own time. Slowly.*

Imagine that astonishing hand –
Nerve, muscle, joint, bone,
Opposable thumbs –

Slowly evolving.
Imagine it moving, independent
Of the soft, warm animal of your body.

Imagine a model of that animal.
Where will you send it? Let it explore
Hazard without risk. Imagine that body,

Mechanical, imbued with intelligence. Yours.

> *There must be some way out of here*
> *With our schemes and dreams and human*
> *Hands-on skills and our teamwork, dear,*
> *And our brave imagination.*

II *Landscape for an Autonomous Vehicle*

Imagine you could send your eyes
On an eight month voyage to a rust-red wasteland –
Parched brick dust, and a wind keener than ice.

At the dry bottom of an ancient lake,
Nothing. Rubble. Stripped stones, pebbles, clay,
The upside-down sky-dome terracotta. Look

And look closer. Imagine

Clues in the sediment. Signatures
In the grit. Inanimate rock –
Stories, locked up. The world is information.

Whose daring will build a machine
Like a tree, or the first green algae, breathing
Itself alive in this snuffed-out desert?

III *Sellafield 'Legacy' Storage Ponds*

Imagine a place on Earth as fierce as this –
As hostile and hazardous as outer space –
Ferocious secrets.

Sludge in the storage ponds.
Liquor in the sump tank.
Cracked concrete. Seeps and leaks.

Spelks, specks, cactus spikes
Of deadly light
Spat out – sly, imperceptible bullets –

Fry cells. Scramble the codes
Driving the beautiful, delicate instruments –
Vital
Instructions for life.

Imagine you could send your eyes, your hands.
Fix the mess. Make amends.
Cancel the legacy. Stop the clocks, rewind

The years, the race, the pulse, the waste, the ponds.

Two Autonomous Vehicles

IV *CARMA*
(Continuous Autonomous Radiometric Monitoring Assistant)

What's this, trundling across
Inaccessible space?

A child's yellow truck, stuttering
Pulses of amplified light,
Bouncing them off an unseen target,

Measuring distance as time.
Range-finder. Map-maker. Game
Straight out of a teenage bedroom,

Avoiding obstacles, plotting
Your route, as an insect might,
Or a small wheeled dinosaur, had

Evolution taken that path, at a crawl
And strangely clumsy, quite
Unaware of yourself, you're the interface

Between two Eras. Oblivious
Of what your uneven autonomous progress
Might mean, you navigate

Between the human and machine – almost
Intelligent.

V *MIRRAX*

(Miniature Robot for Restricted Access Exploration)

A tri-partite cylinder, jointed, I worm
Through a hole in the wall, thin as a limb,
Straight as a die, a long, thin 'I',

Omnidirectional – versatile, nimble, glide
On four independent wheels, weasel my way
In continual metamorphosis, changing form,

Amorphous. Reconfigurable. Taking my shape
To fit the job, as a body should – a sprite, an imp,
An elf – an 'L', a three-sided 'U', raising an arm

Aloft, I-spy. A half-finished sketch of a box.
MIRRAX.
Miraculous. Nothing in nature comes close.

> *Out of the simple complex flows*
> *From sets and tiers of patterns*
> *Engrained in our machines and brains*
> *And our human interactions.*

2 SPACE

I *ADR*

(Active Debris Removal)

Among the constellations of space junk
Wheeling above your head, imagine
A robotic arm with six degrees of freedom –

Its surge, heave, sway, its roll, its pitch and yaw –
Unfolding, a precision instrument, a litter-picker,
Its grasping algorithms and its colour depth sensor;

Strength, dexterity and stiffness. Think of a lobster claw
Snatching its prey in the ocean's dark. How long it takes
To make a hand to lift a cup to drink.

II

Control Architecture, programmer, tele-operator of the obedient
Semi-autonomous Master-Slave Assembly – what are you,
Human? Unpredictable. Fluent,

Adaptable, emotional, creative – often mistaken.
Your charged language sizzles, electric;
The root of your word 'Robotics' stings like a whip.

The time has come to speak of collaboration.

A team is more than its players, dear,
A machine not mere components,
And the complex springs from the simple things
At unexpected moments.

Out of the simple complex flows
From sets and tiers of patterns
Engrained in our machines and brains
And our human interactions.

Crunch; squeeze; grind; grate together.
The world is moving in its own time. Slowly.

III *Sample Analysis on Mars*

It sounds so simple: a search
Like scrabbling for coal,
For carbon compounds

And light elements – hydrogen, oxygen, nitrogen.
A box the size of a microwave oven.
Curiosity is doing it on its own –

Sample analysis on Mars,
A wheel of small cups
Containing scooped soil, drilled rock,

Thimbles of solvent, miniature kilns
Cooking its samples to vapour, the mass spectrometer
Screening them into their elegant tables.

Out of these numbers, worlds flow. The samples,
Ancient clays laid down in oceans, volcanic crystals
Splitting an X-ray beam at specific angles,

Slow oxidation and rust. How simple a process
History is – metamorphosis, minerals, rocks;
And the long road to knowing this – how complex.

IV *Ingenuity Has Photographed Perseverance*

So lonely it looks down there in the rosy desert;
An animal, raising its head,
Slowly gazing about it, seeking its likeness,

The most advanced organisation of parts
Peering into the most primitive.
Ancient microbial life: what does it look like?

The tide has gone out forever, leaving nothing
But sand, grit, stone – and this creature
All on its own, out of place

And time – an arthropod
Dropped down, a dinosaur, tortoise-slow
And deliberate, mirroring something. What do you feel?

Perseverance. Ingenuity. Such noble virtues –
Reason, precision, daring, collaboration – embodied
In wheels, springs, motors and circuits; the drone

Gazing down at it from on high like a god. Surprisingly sad
Its immense solitude,
Tearing the heart that still beats, that is there to be torn.

3 CYBERNETICS

I

Let the mechanical engineer talk to the electrical engineer,
The software architect, logic modeller, evolutionary biologist,
The neuroscientist, bio-engineer, mechanical engineer –

In the great marketplace, trading ideas,
Let them talk, let them listen, let them all converse together.
Grant them inspiration. Let them be inspired by Nature.

II

Who knows where the body ends
And the mind begins?

Let your neural networks grapple with it.
Turn it over in your hands,

Feeling its edges in the dark.
Intelligence is teamwork.

Imagination leaps, darts,
Playfully senses and worms into places

Logic cannot, where the body dare not go,
Its own extension.

III

And the outcomes of actions
Will be inputs for further actions
Says the Controller of the advanced automaton;

And the difference between the actual
And the desired value of a process variable
Is the error signal applied as feedback

Says the complex system
Evolving emergent properties of spontaneous order.

So it's Hey, hey, the logic gates
And the streams of information,
And it's three cheers for your bright ideas
And your flashes of inspiration.

IV *Moon*

Imagine this: a robot on the Moon.

Is it a solar-powered rover, clever wheels
Clambering over boulders, out of holes,

Learning, by reinforcement, to control
Load distribution, traction on loose soils?

Is it a pair of hands, snapping bricks,
Three-D-printed, into walls, houses, habitats?
How does it operate? Does it send signals back

To somebody waiting, maybe an astronaut
Orbiting round it, sharing its eyes, touch, sense
Of orientation, where it is in space?

Is it a beautiful thing, a robot? The Moon?
Human intention? Their interaction, a dance
Moving from tele-operated to autonomous?

Do not try to answer this question. Sometimes a place,
Luminous from a distance, turns out desolate
When you arrive. Beyond the light of the Sun

Worlds that cannot support a life with water or oxygen
Wait for the robots' mapping, drilling, mines.

If we are not there now, we will be. Soon.

V *Human*

Imagine a machine,
Its mobility function excellent over rough terrain.

Its light sensors, complex image recognition,
Memory-mapping in three dimensions,

Twin actuators, manipulators, degrees of dexterity, grip,
Robust enough to flex iron, gentle with eggshells.

Imagine it could not exist in isolation
But only with others like it, linking up

Its system of mirrors, its logic encoded in symbols
Allowing it to reflect on sameness and difference,

Enmeshing it with its other selves in their millions,
Its networks lighting up its habitats, visible from space.

Imagine those networks knitting into one contraption
Entangled with the machinery of a planet

That sends its delicate instruments into orbit,
Weightless as thistledown, to fire back information.

Imagine it gazing at itself from a great distance.
What is that ache? Where is it felt? What does it mean?

Imagine it able to recognise itself from this description.

VI *Autonomous*

How far away they are, out there among the stars,
The machines of the future. Too far to recognise
Bodies, objects, landmarks, unexpected shapes,

Feelings – the sudden dust-storms sweeping across Mars.

The world is moving in its own time. Slowly.

You can see it from space –

An ancient planet. Across its scarred surface
Homes, schools, businesses, offices, cities
Flicker, a brain scan – adaptive, emergent,

Highly-distributed networks,
Connecting together a myriad ways,
Generating synergies.

Do they augment us?
Will they replace us?
What will be lost to us in their implacable reasoning?

For it's Hey, hey, the logic gates
And the streams of information,
And it's three cheers for your bright ideas
And your flashes of inspiration.

VII

The device in your pocket buzzes.
Already it can recognise your face
But it does not know the answer.

It does not know what it knows,
Or what is at stake –
Your privacy. Your job. Your life. Your species.

VIII *I Want to Step Inside You, Computer*

Free in the sunshine, under the trees,
The next generation, fresh out of school – you. Who

Will you become?
The small, the enormous questions.

At night you unpick them while the planet spins,
The stars obscured by the light from a billion screens,

The blinding ice or the burning forest.
What does it mean

To be truly autonomous? Human, machine.

Scroll down the menu: as the world unfurls, fractal,
Endlessly possible, its clever solutions
Filter the choices, determined by pathways

Locked into its software – sets of instructions,
Subtle, invisible as radiation,
Invade us and alter our circuits and networks.

Control and autonomy, Servant, Master,
Body, mind, intelligence – uncomfortable jargon,
Slippery as nature –

Its endless unfolding, relentless self-organisation.
In the evolution of complex systems
The time has come to speak of collaboration.

Out of the simple complex flows
From sets and tiers of patterns
Engrained in our machines and brains
And our human interactions.

A team is more than its players, dear,
A machine not mere components,
And the complex springs from the simple things
At unexpected moments.

So there must be some way out of here:
From our hi-tech kit and human
Hands-on skills and our synergies
And flashes of inspiration.

Yes, there must be some way out of here,
With our hi-tech kit and human
Hands-on skills and our synergies
And our wild imagination.

IX

Have you sent your third eye ahead of you yet
Into Tomorrow?

It's waiting – for your fingers to make a fist,
Locking around your tools, your phone –
The stone-age axe at the end of your wrist.

How long it has taken
Nature to craft that complex contraption
To grip and lift a cup to your lips. But you

Are engineering your own future. You
And the clever machines.
Can you imagine it? Now,

Make it come true.

Wave

Barrelling in from a distant ocean, a storm
No one remembers – boisterous, flinging up foam –

Crashes into a different element. Ours.
The breakers translate their brute weight

Into a trillion trillion glassy bubbles' bells,
Making invisible ripples, vibrating

Ossicle, cilia, scrolled shell,
Lighting up flickering cities, signals

Interpreted in the palpable soft machine
Of fish and bird, and every listening thing,

Until the world is one round radio
Where everything rhymes

With the machinery of star and galaxy, and the minutest
Sea-borne spiral.

Glorious to feel its fetch, its force,
Confusion, complexity, transmuted into noise,

Riot; this glittering, roaring metamorphosis –
The din of the Universe doing without us.

UNDER THE ICE

1 *Unseen*

Earth gazed at itself. A planet in space.
Alien, expressing itself

In incomprehensible languages, hidden
In scales beyond sense.

One voice was Ice.
Earth demanded translation.

Solid ice, thousands of miles wide. Silence. Immense
Creaks, cracks, rumbles. Creeping. Buckled, flexed,
Locked down blue-white rock-ice rivers, compressed,

Each stream a gut, squeezing itself out,
Endlessly replenishing itself. Beneath it,
Its own inaccessible underworld. A continent.

Easier to plant a boot in the Moon's dust
Or explore a distant body in space, than to reach it.

Earth asked each gleaming ice stream, What next?

Flint-hard, miles deep, Ice sealed its answers
Inside its capacious arrangement of elements.

Archives, sediments, signatures. Many secrets.

2 *Float*

Who has locked up three-quarters of the world's fresh water
As if it was rock? A substance

That fractures the rules.
That opens out its delicate hexagonal lattice,
Its spacious lacework, lighter than its liquid.

A solid that floats on its own melt,
Without which the world would not recognise itself.
A solid that flows under its own weight.

That slips, fluid and fluent, between its states.
Whose heft carves continents. Whose vanishing is this:
A single snowflake.

3 *Thwaites*

Glacier, you are a keystone. Behind your ice shelf,
The Western ice sheet rests upon rock
Lower than kelp forests, sponges and sea-stars.

What can you tell us about sudden collapses?

Many rooms deep, the world contradicts itself. Its clocks
Tick fast, slow. Stable, unstable. The present
Grounds on a sea-floor that once knew tree roots.

Sea level. What does it mean? Always provisional.

Slip, slide, glide on your melt-water and sediments,
Ice stream. Accelerate. The great architecture
Sings to itself, argues, negotiates, back and forth,

Circling pulses of temperature, atmosphere, ocean –
Millennia, thousands of miles – an enormous structure,
You at its centre,

Glacier, undercut, thinning, beginning to weaken,

Wobbling on your exquisite tipping-points. Look,
You are coming unpinned
From your dangerous, uncertain, submarine bedrock.

4 *Antarctica Without Its Ice*

Springs back, naked, above the ocean –
Something recovered from the pitch-black remotest
Depths: raddled, ragged, honeycombed old bones.

What has eaten you in the dark, the cold,
The too-many sunsets, your million-year winters?
Chewed you to filigree? An archipelago,

Black vertebrae, worn down, spat out
On a far shore. Too huge. Too much forgotten,
Seamed, scarred, rucked, ripped, pitted, foulbitten –

Unrecognisable, without your great burden.
Volcanoes, molten. Miles high mountains
Rear up out of the sea, disordered, rewritten

Over and over so many times, what is there left
To make sense of? Only
Space. Endless. Pitch-black. Icy. In orbit,

A cold eye opens.

5 *Five Eyes*

Whose eye
Makes this whole vast inaccessible frozen
Difficulty visible

For the first time, at high resolution?
Variations in the snow.
Alterations on the surface.

What questions
Will it ask of the mountains, the satellite
Peering down from its orbit

At glittering granite staring millennia
Into the Sun? At south-facing slopes,
Sunk in persistent shadow?

The mountains are moving
Imperceptibly, warmed and cooled. Whose patient
Eye speeds their slow clock

And, delicate as a bird, from a hundred metres,
Commits them to memory? The drone
Whirrs back to Earth, an ice-launched eye;

While the laser's carefully-levelled eye stipples
Every uneven crack and knobble
With a point of light.

It hauls back each surface in the finest net.
Repeats and repeats. If a pebble works loose,
Memory, pin-sharp and accurate, screens it.

The radar's eye peers
Under the blue ice; slowly,
Painstakingly, unpeels it. Years

Unpack their information, layer
By layer, each wave returning
With a different story. Only

The fifth eye, in its soft machine,
Its delicate networks, can stitch
This picture together – satellite, drone,

Laser, radar – ice field, image, data,
The mountain's minutest movement – and begin
To compute what it means.

6 *Cosmogenic Nuclide*

Beryllium-10, be a window
Into the bedrock, deeply buried
Under exactly how many millennia?

Where the ice sheet conceals its particular
Internal boundaries, be a tell-tale
Down at the trimline.

Subtlest isotope, quartz lattice
Blasted apart by the constant, indelible rain,
What has a star

Shattering, shredding itself in the coldness of space,
To say about this –
When did your bedrock last see daylight?

Little Beryllium-10, to track you down
Takes enormous effort:
Drilled, sieved, crushed, digested in acid,

Accelerated past the spectrometer's magnet.
Will you unfold, from your smallness, immense
Grandeur and grace? –

Be a witness,
Beryllium-10, to the planet's
Slightly imperfect exchange with its star,

Its mildly elliptical, faintly eccentric orbit?
Do you hold in your smallness a clue
To its too-huge secrets?

Most of the time, the world is in hiding.
It reveals itself little by little, Beryllium-10,
Through the narrowest inlet.

7 *Basal Shear*

Earth asked: What is your engine? The ice sheet
Answers with its own weight.
Slow accumulation.

Behind it, more weight. History
Drives it. Below,
Resistance. Drag. Rock. Every kind of argument.

The ice sheet wrestles its nine enormous stresses,
Plastic. Contorted,
Twisted, wrenched out of shape. By what magic

Will it transform itself to swallow
A whole invisible valley of boulders?
Shifting between its twin states, its difficult progress

Down at its dark base fantastically pressured,
It breaks its own locks.
Does not recognise itself.

Now will you report what you slowly enfold,
The burden
You bear to the ocean?

8 *Invisible Mending*

Little transparent beads, buttons, zips,
Glass spokes, spirals, weird seeds, tiny broken
Needles, living fossils, miniature spaceships

Adrift in the far galaxies of our own planet:

What can the monumental machine, huge as the sky,
Its clock of ice ticking down sunlit nights,
Heavy as a mountain, bring you from the nunataks,

Vanishingly tiny spinners of sweetness from sunlight?

Here is the place where ocean and glacier meet.
Bedrock and grounding line. Sediment. Grit.
The green glaze mineral sheen of life, small tools to fix

Troubles so immense, they can't be seen, or spoken,
Bit by invisible bit.

9 *Ice Core*

Who am I, holding my breath, so long
Silent, a prisoner, trapped
In a lattice of ice? I am old
As charcoal and ochre in a dark cave. Deeper:

That no name floated upon, no song
But a shimmer of birds
And all those web-footed, lizard-hipped ones
Whose eulogies, whose secrets,

Fizz on my lips. Whose newsflash, fresh snapshots,
Travel towards you now, down the floating world,
Quick as electricity to a drill-bit, to pop
And sizzle on your tongue, and become words?

10 *Waves*

Ice said: I contain many chronometers.
Counting millennia, long oscillations,
Wave sang to wave, at differing frequencies.

Enormous, infinitesimal
In endless space, a chilled mineral's
Blue iridescence

Locked itself down.
Bent round the Sun,
Space trapped Earth's eccentricities.

So the tides flowed, shrank –
Ice Ages, glacials, interglacials,
Reversible fluctuations, in which

Inhabitants, simple and complex,
Appeared and vanished
In waves, like weather –

Accidents waiting to happen
In the spaces between Ice
And Ice; and the latest

Heard the clocks tick. Plotted precise
Aerial surveillance grids,
The skidoo's careful transects,

Sent down their waves. And waves
Brought back Ice's answers.

11 *Numerical Ice Sheet Modelling*

Ice, you are information.
Many streams. A shimmer of voices.
How do you flow?

Slow sedimentary process.
Snow and sky, firn, pressed down,
Down, squeezed into blue glass.

Thinning. Acceleration. Observation,
Translation. Multiple channels of data.
Abstraction. Mathematical description.

A grid on a screen in three dimensions.
Time, change, uncertainties
Rippling through it.

All the fixed forces, all the variables,
Known, unknown, tuned and calibrated,
Validated, compared with the Actual –

Grainy aerial radar echo,
Ice core. Sediment sample –
Ever more accurate. The model,

The beautiful model: here is the ocean,
Ice, into which all observation –
Sensing, physical and remote, your multiple

Glittering streams of information – flow.

12 *Melt*

Come back as images, echoes. Sing of an alien
Planet – this one,
That comforts itself in its own language – water,

Gracefully shifting between its estates,
Snapping, slipping, out of its body, liquid to vapour,
Ice sheet to ocean, freeze and flow.

All that intricate locking and unlocking.
Green cells and sunlight and little bubbles –
Recycled carbon and oxygen, going round again

And again. All those invisible rivers.
Those immense libraries of stone.

All that action and reaction, changing, exchanging –
Loosening, tightening, shifting, shaping, making, remaking,

Small and large negotiations with light;
The capture, store and release of a star's heat;
The long, irregular breathing. In and out.

On the other side of the world,

High, high up in the roaring, clear strata,
Miles above shimmering deserts, mountains, ocean,
Roll the vast eddies.

Positives and negatives. Surpluses, deficits.
Enormous, complicated fiscal adjustments.

Far away, the Ice hears it.

Deep, salt, warm ocean currents
Hauled south, wheeled round, well up
Where wind and fresh melt-water drag them.

Slow. Slow. Hollowed, undercut. Cut
To the grounding line, the great Buttress
Answers Earth's question.

13 *Remote Sensing*

Sometimes the world understands itself from very close.
Its tiniest fractions, elements and isotopes,
Splay out their waves. Who will interpret
The alphabet interleaved in the ice core's couplets?

Sometimes the world must drill down into its grit,
Winch it up, measure its heft in its palm.
Sometimes the cold weight of its past must rest on its skin.

And sometimes its eye is frozen to a screen.
Sometimes the world peers back at itself from a great distance,
Snapping its endless selfies, firing them down
In waves to disembodied listening devices.

Then, where its own soft body cannot pass,
Sometimes it sends down its waves to sound its own secrets –
Slow, slow accumulations of data, patient as ice –

Streams within streams, multiple speeds, ribbons,
Temperature, pressure, gravity, drag, slide,

Twisted bands of cobalt blue, marbled with white.
Ice slates, schists, ice gneisses. Ice, ubiquitous

In the Universe, a permanent presence,
What are you doing, so close to the Sun? Recycling,

I have forgotten its name, a planet in space.

NOTES

NOTES

These are notes to the poems; where they refer to science, they provide only my own limited understanding of it, intended to illuminate the poetry. I have not included many written references: much of the information was gleaned either from conversations with the scientists thanked in the Acknowledgements, from organisations like the British Trust for Ornithology and the British Antarctic Survey, or from *New Scientist* magazine and website. I hope that readers will forgive my own errors and be inspired to follow up the science in more detail.

How the Fishes Listen (13). According to palaeontologists and scientists studying bioacoustics, the sense of hearing evolved from structures in the inner ear of bony fishes which appeared on the planet around 415 million years ago. Its development depended upon 'hair cells' (the basilar papilla) and particles of calcium carbonate called 'otoliths', structures used for balance and to detect motion. These are contained in the ears both of fish and of advanced mammals such as humans. Otoliths have the same chemical composition as Carboniferous limestone. Human ears are thought to have evolved from gills.

Ingredients (14). This and the previous poem are part of a sequence written for BBC Radio 4, 'Susurrations of the Sea', produced by Julian May in 2022. This sequence playfully explores a duality of scale, from the sea's tiniest sounds to its immense bass roar, and uses this as an auditory metaphor to consider the enormous planetary processes from which small, local phenomena emerge. In particular, the sequence touches recurrently on the oceans' role in Earth's 'carbon cycle' and temperature regulation.

Carbon dioxide in Earth's atmosphere, which absorbs heat and radiates it back to Earth, is essential to prevent the planet from freezing. Natural processes like wild fires and volcanic eruptions release carbon dioxide into the atmosphere. So do human activities, especially burning fossil fuels like coal, oil and natural gas. Research from ice cores, rock samples and satellites, explored in detail at the end of *Rhizodont* in 'Under the Ice', shows that, since the beginning of the Industrial Revolution in the 18th century, human activities have raised atmospheric carbon dioxide by nearly 50%. The graph of this atmospheric carbon dioxide correlates with that of Earth's rising temperatures.

To some extent, the oceans help to mitigate this warming effect. This poem refers to one of the ways in which that happens. Carbon dioxide dissolves in water and phytoplankton convert the carbon into sugars. In the same way that plants support life on land, phytoplankton supports marine life. That life in turn contributes to the immensely slow geological processes by which the oceans lock up some carbon dioxide in carbon-rich rocks such as chalk and limestone – the 'ingredients' of this poem.

On a more measurable timescale, the oceans also act as a heat sink. The oceans heat up through energy transfer from the atmosphere. Cold water can hold more dissolved carbon dioxide than warm water, so cold sea water at the Poles absorbs carbon dioxide. The cold water travels along deep ocean currents, which are driven by the difference in density between warm and cold water or salt and fresh water. Once they reach the warmer areas elsewhere on the planet, centuries later, they heat up, and rise, releasing carbon dioxide back into the atmosphere in a cyclical process. These 'pulses' of currents are explored at the end of the book, in 'Under the Ice'.

BOOK I: CARBONIFEROUS

Tinkers' Fires (17). In the 1960s the word 'Tinker' was the common term used for travellers who specialised in mending pots and pans. Today some people find it offensive. It is used in this poem alongside other colloquial terms for traveller people from the local dialect. The poem is a memory from that time of traveller families passing through East Durham pit villages. Some mining families in those villages were related to traveller families, and both horse trading and pot mending took place during those visits.

Kittycouldhavebeen (18). Another personal memory from East Durham.

The poems on pages 20–27 about the Durham coast were commissioned by the National Trust's People's Landscape project and

128

New Writing North for the Durham Book Festival in 2019. They focus on the regeneration of Durham's 'black beaches'. The Carboniferous coal measures lie beneath younger rock on the Durham coast, so the deep mines needed to extract it were among the latest to be sunk. For decades, until the last of them closed in 1993, the sea shore between Seaham and Hartlepool was despoiled with waste dumped from those pits. There followed from 1997 to 2000 a massive, multi-agency clean-up operation called 'Turning the Tide', which removed 1.3 million tonnes of colliery spoil from the beaches and created a coastal footpath. I was poet-in-residence for that project, and wrote about it in poems published in *Two Countries* (Bloodaxe Books, 2014). A generation later the coast is designated an Area of Outstanding Natural Beauty. But the former mining communities of Horden and Easington Colliery are still beset with social problems rooted in the pit closures. I wrote these poems in response to visits to those communities, during which I talked with young people who had no memory of the coalmining past. Their words inform these poems. All names have been changed to preserve anonymity.

Tiny Lights (20). Glow-worms, rare in North-East England, have been found in one of the wooded denes near Horden.

Wildlife (21). Three poems based on conversations with children from Years 5 and 6, Cotsford Junior School, Horden. The poems quote the children's words. 'Easington's Pit Cage' is a reference to the rectangular black pit cage which stands as a hill-top memorial overlooking the former Easington Colliery site. The Numbered Streets are an area of terraced housing in Horden particularly known for social problems. Limekiln Gill is a wildlife sanctuary and a site favoured by glue-sniffers.

A Short Walk from the Sea's Edge (24). This poem has two epigraphs. The first is the title of a poem by the Caribbean poet Derek Walcott. The second, which also closes this poem, is a quotation from 'Fantasia on a Theme of James Wright', by Sean O'Brien, from his collection, *The Drowned Book* (Picador, 2007).

Speckled Wood (27). This poem was inspired by the involvement of Easington Brownies and Guides in the Hawthorn Dene Heritage

Project, 'a cross-generational sharing through film, photography and testimony', supported by the Heritage Lottery Fund and run by Sharon Bailey, Ellin Hare and Nicola Balfour from The Barn at Easington. This wonderful project gave children cameras and allowed them to explore the landscape of Hawthorn Dene through its people, stories and living creatures.

Hermeneutics (28). A poem commissioned for the Women40 project, Trinity Hall, Cambridge (2016), which celebrated 40 years since the college first accepted female undergraduates. I was a History undergraduate at Trinity Hall in 1979. I wanted my East Durham ancestors to know how things have changed for women over the last century. A 'pit-yacker' is someone who speaks Pitmatic, the vanished dialect of North-East collieries.

Wooden Doll (29). The Wooden Doll is a larger than life female figure which stands outside the Prince of Wales tavern on Customs House Quay above the Tyne in North Shields. She is the latest in a series. The first Wooden Doll was a ship's figurehead, placed there in 1814. She was used as a bollard to drag heavy masts and gear up the banks of the Quay, and it became a custom for sailors to cut slivers from her for good luck. There have been several replacements, the latest of which was installed in 1992. The poem considers the unwritten histories of women in the Shields area, from brewers and publicans to fishwives and bait gatherers. It was written for the pamphlet, *The Wooden Dollies of North Shields*, ed. Keith Armstrong and Peter Dixon, 2018. The Black Middens are a group of notorious rocks at the mouth of the Tyne.

Saa't (30). From the early 19th century until the mid 20th century the North Sea herring industry flourished. Women were employed by herring yards to gut and pack herring into barrels with salt for export to the Baltic. Season by season, these 'herrin' lasses' followed the shoals as they travelled south from Shetland in spring to Great Yarmouth in October. This poem, written in the Northumbrian language, is based on interviews with women from Northumberland and Shetland, and describes the hard work, independence and camaraderie which they remembered. It was written for *Herring Our Joy*, a CD of songs from the herring industry produced by American folksinger Mary Garvey in 2021.

Low Light (32). This ballad was inspired by a conversation with Sheila Hirsch at the Old Low Light fishing heritage centre, North Shields. The Low Light was a leading mark for vessels entering the River Tyne. Sheila is believed to have been the first female trawler skipper in the UK, and her 27 years at sea took her all over Britain and to the USA. In fishing culture it was considered bad luck for a woman even to set foot on a boat. Among her many adventures, Sheila worked aboard deep sea trawlers. R. Irvin and Sons, originally based at North Shields, operated a very successful fleet of deep sea trawlers named after Scottish mountains, and so prefixed with the word 'Ben'. Sheila is now retired and volunteers for the North Shields Fishermen's Heritage Project. Fishing remains one of the most dangerous occupations in the country, and this ballad is dedicated to everyone who has lost someone at sea. It has been set to music and sung by Celia Bryce.

Shields Gut (34). Set on the North Shields Fish Quay ('the Gut'), this poem explores the complexities of Brexit for the fishing community. Most fishermen opposed UK involvement in the EU because, for decades, the EU Common Fisheries Policy was a disaster both for fishing and for the environment. Species quota and size regulations intended to prevent overfishing led to the scandalous waste of millions of tonnes of edible fish. Because they could not be legally landed, fish caught in indiscriminate nets were routinely thrown back, dead: a practice which fishermen rightly considered a criminal waste.

The poem refers to the history of the area around the Fish Quay, including historic gun emplacements, notably Clifford's Fort, a battery from the Anglo-Dutch wars of the 17th century, and the earlier 'Spanish Battery', supposedly named after Spanish mercenaries who manned it for Henry VIII during his planned invasion of Scotland. Admiral Lord Collingwood's memorial reminds us of the Anglo-French wars of the early 19th century, while many North Shields trawlers and drifters were conscripted for minesweeping and reconnaissance duties against German warships during both the 20th century's World Wars. In contrast to the fishermen's sentiments about the EU, the poem highlights the increasingly multicultural neighbourhood around the Fish Quay, the international nature of employment and markets, and pressing global issues such as migration and environmental concerns. 'Shields

Gut' and the previous poem, 'Low Light', were written for *Tyne Anew*, ed. Keith Armstrong and Peter Dixon (Northern Voices, 2019).

The Bird Roads (35-50): This poem sequence was commissioned in 2020-21 by Amble Development Trust for the Bord Waalk sculpture trail from Low Hauxley to Warkworth, which opened in 2023. Each poem focuses on one or more bird species from the coast. Each is part of a series of six site-specific podcasts, a collaboration with audio artist Geoff Sample, which also includes Geoff's recordings of local voices and wildlife. The podcasts are available via the free Bord Waalk App. Geoff was an important source of information about birds for this project. So was Mark Cocker's *Birds and People* (Cape, 2013).

The first poem, **Passage Migrants** (35), focuses on the bird species which rest and feed temporarily on the shore while on migration, especially in autumn. Some, like turnstones and sandpipers, are fairly common species, and may stay for the winter. The name 'stint' was used locally for small waders like these. Others, like whimbrels and redwings, pass through regularly; and some are just occasional vagrants. The poem places these wanderers in a wide context of geological time. It refers to the Hauxley to Amble foreshore, which crosses over Carboniferous rocks from the Middle and Lower Pennine Coal Measures Formations, 320–310 million years old. It also refers to the Pleistocene epoch, which spans the Earth's most recent period of glaciations, to the end of the last Ice Age around 11,700 years ago.

Northern Wheatear (37). Wheatears are among the first summer migrants to arrive, so a welcome messenger of spring. Often seen in March in the dunes or on the wall of a coastal field, the wheatear is conspicuous with a large white rump patch, which gives the bird its name (from 'white arse'). As the poem suggests, wheatears have been landing on the Low Hauxley sea shore for many thousands of years.

Low Hauxley is an important, multi-layered archaeological site. The footprints of wild animals and humans who inhabited the area around 7,000 years ago have been identified in peat exposed on the shore. A community-based team of archaeologists led by

Clive Waddington recorded them, and Waddington showed in his book *Rescued from the Sea* (2014) that the area was wooded or forested at that time. His team also discovered an extensive scatter of Late Mesolithic flints near Low Hauxley, on top of a thick storm surge deposit which is thought to have been caused by a tsunami resulting from the Storegga underwater landslide about 8,200 years ago. This event would have inundated significant parts of a low-lying area called Doggerland, which intermittently connected what is now Britain's North Sea coast to North-West Europe.

Later prehistoric remains identified by Waddington at Low Hauxley include dune burials which indicate the presence of the first metal workers from around 2,400 BCE, and a slightly later Bronze Age cemetery. This and the next two poems allude to the long occupation of the site, as well as to traces of the recent coalmining legacy which can still be found on the shore, and to the concrete remains of World War II coastal defences.

Tudelum (38). 'Tudelum' was a Northumbrian fishermen's word for a small wader like a redshank or a turnstone. The name echoes the birds' call. This poem refers to the birds' footprints in the sand, reflected in the motifs knitted into local fisher 'ganseys' (woollen jerseys), and in the funeral pots of the Beaker People buried here more than 4,000 years ago. A 'cist' is a stone-lined burial chamber. Bondicar is a rock south-east of Hauxley Haven. 'Carr' is an Old Northumbrian or possibly Celtic word meaning a rock. The poem reflects on Low Hauxley's layers of archaeology, stretching back to the 7,000 year old footprints in the peat, and the longer relation between humans and birds. Flutes made from bird bones found in southern Germany are the oldest known musical instruments, dating back 40,000 years.

Sand Martins (39). As you walk along the shore between Low Hauxley and Amble you will see the layer of exposed peat beneath the sand dunes. This is part of the same layer exposed on the beach, described above. This poem refers to the people who left those footprints 7,000 years ago. The sand martin is a migratory bird which winters south of the Sahara, and arrives on our shores to nest in colonies in holes which the birds dig out of sand banks. The word 'shuttle' refers to a tool used in net-making from prehistoric times to the present day. The implication is that birds such as sand martins and their near relatives house martins have shared their territories and survival instincts with humans for many thousands of years.

Bloody Cranesbill (40). If you follow the coastal path along the dunes between Low Hauxley and Amble from May to October, you will see the unmistakable magenta blossoms of Northumberland's county flower, the bloody cranesbill. This plant loves limestone soils and sandy dunes. The geranium family, to which it belongs, derives its name from the Greek word for the crane, as the plant's long seed pods were thought to resemble that bird's bill. The flower attracts many kinds of insect. The poem was inspired by the naturalist Mark Cocker, who writes movingly of the transfer of energy in the natural world. Plants absorb certain wavelengths of sunlight for photosynthesis to create sugars, which feed invertebrates, which in turn feed birds; so the skylark's and meadow pipit's songs are literally, in Mark's words, 'sunlight made audible'. Hawkbit, with its yellow dandelion-like flower, is another common plant of these dunes. It is part of the sunflower family and was once believed to be eaten by hawks to improve their eyesight.

Cormorant (41). Cormorants are often seen perching with their wings outstretched on the old jetties and abandoned staithes at Amble, the harbour town at the mouth of the River Coquet. Amble is now Northumberland's main fishing port, but until 1969 it was dominated by coal export. An extensive rail network linked the inland collieries at Radcliffe and Broomhill to its staithes. Here, the iridescent black cormorant is compared to coal. Fabled for its greed, it is likened to a dinosaur, and its prehistoric outline brings to mind a vast timescale, encompassing the drowned forest of Hauxley's Mesolithic past, and possibly dramatic future developments brought about by climate change.

Cubby (42). The eider duck is known locally as 'Cubby', 'Cuddy's' or 'St Cuthbert's duck', after the Anglo-Saxon saint who became Bishop of Lindisfarne in 684 CE. This poem is written in a language spoken by fishermen on the north Northumberland coast two or three generations ago. That language was a direct descendant of the Anglian speech that was widely spoken throughout most of central and northern Britain in St Cuthbert's time. Female eiders gather in small groups for protection, to raise their ducklings communally without the drakes. Young females without offspring often join them and are known as 'aunties'. The poem compares these strongly defined male and female roles, and communal behaviour, with the close community of an old-style fishing village.

Birds (43). In 2022, according to the British Trust for Ornithology, 43% of regularly occurring bird species in Britain were classed as threatened, with another 10% near-threatened. 23 bird species were classified as critically endangered. Amble is a place of continual change, where the river has dramatically altered course, and industries (like coal export and the brickworks) have come and gone. Its wildlife has changed, too. Bird species like the corncrake have vanished from the surrounding fields, while new species like the little egret have moved in along the river. Even the local language is changing: words like 'pickies' for terns, and 'creeves' for crab and lobster pots, are disappearing. Birds are so entwined with our daily life, our thoughts and dreams, that to imagine them gone is somehow also to presage our own demise.

Fog (45). The foghorn's moan was once a characteristic sound of the British coast. In the past, the Coquet Gun was fired from Coquet Island lighthouse every three minutes in fog. Today an automatic electronic fog signal sounds a three-second blast every 30 seconds. Most vessels now use radar and no longer rely solely on the foghorn for navigation in poor visibility.

Wishbone (46). This poem was inspired by objects washed up along the tideline near Amble Harbour. In bird anatomy, the 'wishbone' or 'furculum' acts as a spring that aids flight by pushing the shoulders apart during the downstroke of the wings. Ancient Greeks, Etruscans, Romans and other ancient cultures used birds as oracles and their bones for divination. The relics of some of these beliefs remain as superstitions. In previous generations, fishing communities were particularly superstitious about birds. Feathers were considered bad luck, and burning them was worse still. Some beliefs had an empirical basis. Gulls circling at height were thought to presage bad weather; such behaviour could be the result of air pressure changes.

'Wishbone' explores the cultural significance of birds, like the

Arctic tern, whose arrival back from the Antarctic each spring 'keeps the world's clock ticking'. 'Tirrick', 'tarree', 'teerum' and 'pickie' are all Northumbrian names for various kinds of tern, including the rare Roseate tern which breeds on Coquet Island. The poem celebrates the Arctic tern's epic journey. According to scientists at Newcastle University, one recent round trip between Northumberland and the terns' Antarctic winter roost was recorded at 59,650 miles.

Many things mentioned in the poem are disappearing: Northumbrian words, like 'merrythowt', 'plotin', 'whew' and 'gripe'; the traditional Northumbrian fishing boat, the coble; even the old Amble fishermen, who would congregate at the boatyard where cobles were built. These distinctive aspects of the place are becoming extinct, like the allosaurus, a bipedal dinosaur that lived about 150 million years ago. The allosaurus belonged to a family called Theropods, from which modern birds evolved, and its skeleton also had a furculum, which is thought to have helped it maintain its upright posture. The poem juxtaposes recent cultural evolution with this enormous timescale, and asks what we, with our plastic waste, will leave behind us.

Linnets (47). These small seed-eating birds thrive in the gorse and other shrubbery along the Northumberland coast. Their sing-song calls can be heard almost all year round. Linnets flock together in colder months on rough ground at the edge of Amble. Although to some people thistles and long grass are 'untidy', they provide ideal habitat for wildlife. This poem touches on the fact that the river's course and sea level have changed dramatically over the centuries, and are only ever provisional.

The Braid (48). 'The Braid' is the name given to the wide green area of regenerated land on the north side of Amble. Until the early 1970s, it was the town's rubbish tip. It was then filled with soil and grassed over, the Guilder's Burn or 'Gut' which crosses it was channelled and, as a marina was created out of the river basin, more land was reclaimed. This poem explores the Braid's importance to Amble residents as a place of recreation and wildlife. It refers to the boatyard, formerly part of J. & J. Harrisons', which was known for building traditional wooden fishing cobles. The last Northumbrian coble was built around 1990. Amble Boat Company took over the yard, building modern vessels from contemporary materials. A new apartment block recalls the site's history in its name, 'Coble Quay'.

Grey Heron (49). This poem is set on the tidal stretch of the River Coquet, between Amble and Warkworth. The Coquet rises in the Cheviot Hills, on the Border between Scotland and England, and over the course of 55 miles it links that wild upland landscape, with its traditional sheep-farming culture, to the sea. Historically the estuary was known for its medieval salt pans and ancient salmon fishery. A 'stell' is a circular stone shelter for sheep (the same word is used for salmon nets), and 'smolt' are young salmon, making their first journey downriver.

Atlantic salmon have a remarkable life-cycle, leaving the river to feed in the Arctic waters around Greenland, before they return a few years later to spawn in exactly the same gravel bed where they were hatched. This cycle has continued since the last Ice Age, and so presumably has the grey heron's watchful hunt. In recent times salmon numbers have declined dramatically. Conservation measures include a fish pass in the weir between Amble and Warkworth, which allows returning salmon to swim upstream, and the controversial closure of the net fishery at sea. Until 2019 salmon fishing was an important part of the Amble fishermen's year but it has now been banned. Many estuarine birds – not just herons, but little egrets, goosanders, cormorants and others – eat young salmon. This poem places the timeless drama of the 'prehistoric' grey heron against Amble's history, first as a coal port then as a salmon fishing harbour, and depicts the bird as an explorer, venturing into Amble's still-to-be-decided future.

The Auld Watter (50). Until it abruptly changed course in March 1765, the River Coquet reached the sea at Birling, about a mile north of its present estuary, and the remains of a medieval harbour are thought to lie under what is now Warkworth Golf Course. The salt marsh occupying the area behind Helsay Point, between the old harbour and the present estuary, is still known locally as 'the Auld Watter'. It is a mysterious landscape, haunted by the curlew's cry.

Full Tide on the Coquet (51). This is the last poem in the 'Bird

Roads' sequence. Barnacle geese pass over in autumn or spring on their way to and from the Solway. Their migration from their breeding grounds in Greenland and Svalbard in Northern Russia is now well known but in the past seemed so mysterious, it was believed that the geese hatched from barnacles at sea. The poem captures a moment of transition one autumn evening, as barnacle geese fly in across the road and river, to settle on the far shore. There seems something other-worldly in their call and their long, flowing lines in the sky, hence the reference to cuneiform, one of the earliest written scripts. The arrival of geese from places where the ice is melting reminds us of the interconnectedness of the planet, and brings intimations of climate change, and the potential for further flooding.

Can (52). This poem is set on the beach next to Newton Point, between Craster and Beadnell. The word 'sneuk' means a promontory. This is one of the poems which first led the artist Paul Kenny to contact me in 2017. Paul has very kindly allowed me to use one of his images for the cover of this book.

Off Beadnell Point (53). Another poem from the 'Susurrations of the Sea' sequence, touching on the sea's role in geological deposition and erosion, the oceans' properties as a heat sink, and their place in Earth's carbon cycle.

Sandylowper (54). 'Sandylowper' was the Beadnell fishermen's word for the sand-hopper, a tiny crustacean which feeds on dead seaweed along the tideline and which in turn provides vital fuel for shorebirds. Sandylowpers themselves probably evolved around 150 million years ago, but their family, Crustacea, predates Northumberland's Carboniferous rocks by hundreds of millions of years. Chitin is the material from which their exoskeletons are formed. The poem was inspired by watching sand-hoppers fleeing onto a tarmac road ahead of a tidal surge in 2015.

A Lang Way Hyem (55–66). This long sequence originated as a radio-poem, a collaboration with producer Adam Fowler and presenter Anna Scott-Brown for their BBC Radio 4 series, *Conversations on a Bench* (2016). It was inspired by interviews which Anna conducted on a bench overlooking Beadnell harbour. The bench, with its serpent-head ironwork, is used by visitors and residents. Anna met holidaymakers, conservation officers and environmental scientists, and some members of the village's last remaining fishing families. The radio-poem was a close dialogue between the verse and the interviews, with a connecting chant made up of salmon-netting terms, berths and superstitions. It contained much longer interview extracts and many more interviewees than this version. Here, I have taken the liberty of including heavily-edited excerpts from some of the interviews, in order to give a sense of the dialogue structure, and how the poetry borrows from the speech. I am greatly indebted to Anna, Adam and the interviewees for this.

Beadnell harbour was once a thriving point of export for lime. This was produced from limestone quarried in the village and fired in the kilns, just behind where the bench now stands. The village was also known historically for its summer herring industry and its traditional coble boats used for salmon, crab pots and line fishing. The poem marks one of the last salmon seasons in the village, as salmon-netting was banned on the Northumberland coast in 2019.

Today Beadnell has one of the highest percentages of holiday homes in Britain, and its industries are tourism and leisure. The poem responds to the human 'incomers' who ebb and flow, referring to the cyclical migration of Beadnell's wild creatures and the pre-historic nature of its seashore. The migration of salmon to Arctic waters, of swallows to sub-Saharan Africa, and of Arctic terns to Antarctica, reveals that even the smallest place is connected to a much wider world. So the poem evokes the cycles of seasons and millennia, a history of human migration crystallised within a disappearing dialect, and the constant re-creation of communities, landscapes and ways of being.

'A Lang Way Hyem' means 'a long way home'. Featherblaa' is the name of the biggest dune in Beadnell Bay. The Long Nanny is a small river which divides the Bay, and provides a nesting site for Arctic and little terns. The name 'Nanny' is associated with a Brythonic or early Celtic word, which pre-dates Anglo-Saxon settlement: in Welsh, the related word 'nant' means 'stream'.

Goldcrests (67). Britain's smallest bird, the goldcrest, arrives in large numbers from Scandinavia and the near Continent every autumn and stays until spring. The arrival of a flock is an almost magical experience, as they flit among the leaf-shadows, transforming the garden with their nearly subliminal calls.

Arguments (68). This poem from the 'Susurrations' sequence includes scraps of the Beadnell fishermen's vanishing language, a fossil record of past waves of migration and settlement. 'Lipper', meaning short, choppy waves, is of Old Norse origin. 'Hobble' and its variants, meaning a rolling sea, is from the Dutch. 'Gurrelly', meaning heavy seas, is Dutch or Germanic. Like much Northumbrian fishing language, the sea's 'brek' – where it breaks – is from Anglo-Saxon. For more information on etymology, please see Bill Griffiths, *Fishing and Folk* (Northumbria, 2008).

The Long Line (69–72). This sequence was also written as an audio collaboration, this one with composer Peter Zinovieff. It is a memorial to the fishing communities of the Northumberland coast, who for centuries worked the 'long lines' from their cobles. This type of fishing involved an intimate, sustainable relation to nature, but came at a terrible cost, especially to women, whose unpaid job it was to bait 1,400 hooks a day with mussels gathered from the rocks. The first engines were introduced into Beadnell's sailing cobles in 1918, when Thomas 'Skee' Hall fitted his boat *Golden Horn* with a motor car engine. This marked the beginning of mechanisation for cobles on this part of the coast, which eventually freed women, but which also had wider, ultimately unsustainable, consequences. P.70 of the poem describes a coble being launched by a group of fishermen with the chant, 'Howway, HOOP!' 'The Long Line' was commissioned as an audio installation for Historic England's Immortalised exhibition in London in 2018. Zinovieff's electronic soundscape was based on my archive recordings of Beadnell voices, and derived its instrumental sounds from a traditional Northumbrian folksong sung by retired fisherman John Dixon.

A Hut a Byens (73). This poem and the next were written in response to a commission from Newcastle Centre for the Literary Arts (NCLA) and the Bamburgh Bones project. This archaeological project featured the remains of more than a hundred Anglo-Saxon skeletons, exhumed from the Bowl Hole cemetery beneath Bamburgh Castle, and re-interred in the ossuary in the crypt of St Aidan's Church. Analysis shows that their origins were as diverse as North

Africa, Scandinavia and the Mediterranean. 'A Hut a Byens' is written in the north Northumbrian coastal dialect, as spoken within living memory, and which, as previously noted, was a direct descendant of the Anglian speech of the time of St Cuthbert. Although that dialect is now almost extinct, traces remain, 'buried' or 'fossilised' in local words and place names.

The Tide Clock (75). This nursery rhyme, also commissioned for the Bamburgh Bones project, was inspired by the (possibly Anglo-Saxon) 'tide' or 'mass clock' marking the divine offices, which is incorporated into the wall of the 12th-century St Aidan's church crypt. The church 'hours' were divided into eight, including a night service, Matins. Here Matins is conflated with the early morning service, Lauds. Each verse contains a local reference, explained in the glossary. The 'sky-serpent' is a flock of lapwings following the plough, and refers to the legend of the 'Laidly Wyrm'. 'The spuggie' refers to the famous parable from St Bede's *Ecclesiastical History*, where one of King Oswald's chief men compares human life to a sparrow flying through a window into a lighted hall and out again the other side. This image of life's impermanence has, paradoxically, lasted 1,400 years.

The Fulmar (77). This beautiful grey and white seabird is related to the albatross. It nests on cliffs, including the whinstone on which Dunstanburgh, Bamburgh and Holy Island Castles stand. Gliding on stiff wings, the fulmar is wonderfully aerodynamic, but finds it difficult to land in a strong wind.

Many Hands (78–93): This poem sequence was written in 2017 in response to a commission from the Peregrini Lindisfarne Land-scape Partnership. This was a three-year project supported by the Heritage Lottery Fund, which made possible a wide variety of conservation and community projects across Holy Island and the adjacent mainland, drawing upon heritage, history and biodiversity. The name 'Peregrini' refers to the itinerant monks who first sought refuge on Lindisfarne in 634 CE. The word 'pilgrim' is derived from it. The sequence frequently alludes to the knot-work designs of the famous Lindisfarne Gospels. Throughout, the poems draw on the words of project volunteers.

The Old Lifeboat House (78). Holy Island's old lifeboat house on the western shore was built in 1884 and served until 1925. For generations, until it was withdrawn in 1968, the lifeboat was important to every life on the Island, and within the Island community strong family links remain with those who served on it. The old lifeboat house was given to Holy Island Development Trust by the Crossman family and restored with Heritage Lottery Fund support in 2015. It is now a small museum. The poem explores what have, at times, been delicate relations between Islanders and 'incomers' – both on Holy Island itself and more widely. Hobthrush is a local name for St Cuthbert's Island, a tiny rocky outcrop of Holy Island where St Cuthbert sought isolation. 'The sea-worm with many legs' is an image of the community launching the lifeboat.

Many Hands (79). During World War II, the Danish cargo vessel *Prins Knud* beached on Holy Island's north shore. When mainland experts failed to move her, the Islanders spent six weeks digging a channel to free the stranded vessel: an example of how a small community, working together, can achieve seemingly impossible things.

Gleaners (80). This poem refers to the Island's 19th-century industries: first, herring, with its red-sailed keelboats and itinerant Scottish herring lasses, then quarrying and lime-burning. At that time the Island was crossed by horse-drawn waggonways, transporting limestone to various kiln sites. Finally, it refers to the lime-workers' cottages, excavated as part of the Peregrini community archaeology project. It is difficult to imagine the noise, dirt and activity of those vanished industries on the Island now. The Popple Well provided much of the village's water until the 1950s. Kennedy was the site of some of the Island's limekilns.

Philadelphia (81). The poem refers to a small, abandoned settlement at Cocklawburn on the mainland, serving a former 19th-century limeworks. The ramp to the old limekilns nearby is topped by a World War II gun emplacement. 'The German Ocean' was an old name for the North Sea. 'Pancheek' was a fishing shiel in the area, and the neighbouring settlement of Sandbanks was excavated as a Peregrini community archaeology project. The name 'Philadelphia' means 'brotherly love'.

Gateway (82). Alongside its celebrated Christian heritage, Holy Island is marked by centuries of military history, evident in its 16th-century castle, and 17th-century harbour defences at Osborne's Fort. Peregrini volunteers worked to restore Osborne's Fort as part of a project to conserve buildings of historic interest. Haematite or 'kidney ore', known locally as 'keel', was excavated on the Island in the 18th century, and exported to the Carron iron works, a Scottish foundry at the forefront of the Industrial Revolution, famous for its naval guns.

Red List Species (83). *Dianthus deltoides* or 'Maiden Pink' is one of the Northumberland Red Data Book endangered wildflower species growing on the Heugh, the Whin Sill outcrop on the Island's south shore. The Whin Sill is an intrusive band of igneous dolerite which outcrops across Northumberland, notably on the central part of Hadrian's Wall, at Dunstanburgh Castle, the Farne Islands, Bamburgh, and at the southern end of Holy Island. It is harder than the sedimentary rocks around it. The poem reflects on the astonishing 'sequence of accidents' that has allowed Life to evolve on Earth, and this particular wild flower to survive in this place.

Absences (84). Peregrini's community volunteering project included the 'heritage skill' of drystone walling. The poem lists the names of a number of traditional Island families, and refers to some of the 'marks' they handed down the generations to locate their fishing grounds. For example, 'Bebbla' is Beblowe, the old name for the castle mound, and 'Wingate', traditionally lined up with it, is a mark in the Kyloe hills on the mainland.

Woven (85). The willow sculpture mentioned in this poem was one of several created by Anna Turnbull and Peregrini volunteers as part of a nature trail on the Island. A 'kedge' is an anchor.

Beblowe (86). The poem's title is the name of the castle mound, part of the Island's Whin Sill outcrop. The poem refers to some of the many whin grassland species, and reflects on the varied identities of some of the Island's historic 'blow-in' settlers, which include Irish and Scottish monks, Scandinavian invaders, Irish quarrymen and Scottish herring workers.

Anonymous (87). This poem refers to the graffiti cleaned off the Cocklawburn gun emplacement by Peregrini volunteers, to the bird hide at Lough Pond, and to Anna Turnbull and the Peregrini volunteers' willow sculptures on the Island.

Dig (88). A community archaeology project led by Richard Carlton on the Heugh in summer 2017 revealed an important discovery: a possible Anglo-Saxon church, which could provide a tangible link to Northumbria's first Christian settlers. Connecting ancient faith to a modern quest for spiritual understanding, the poem mentions Seoul, the capital of South Korea, a leader in internet technology, and Cupertino in California's Silicon Valley, which is the home of Apple's HQ.

Arctic Terns (89). As has already been noted, Arctic terns have the longest migration route of any bird. Both Arctic and rare little terns breed on the Island's North Shore. As migrants, terns could themselves be described as 'Peregrini'. The Northumbrian words 'skeer' and 'carr' refer to outcrops of rock.

Begin Again (91). This poem was written to thank the Peregrini volunteers upon whose voices and activities the poems in this sequence are based. It recalls the prehistoric footprints discovered in the peat at Low Hauxley.

Cocklawburn (92). Cocklawburn beach lies between Berwick-upon-Tweed and Lindisfarne National Nature Reserve. This poem was inspired by Ian Kille's Northumbrian Earth walks for Peregrini volunteers, and by photographs of sand, silica crystals and coccoliths, viewed through a microscope lens. The coccoliths, calcium carbonate shells of single-celled protozoa, make another appearance in 'Organic' (96), in Book II.

#rhizodont (93). The fossil of a 'Sarcopterygian' (flesh-finned or lobe-finned) fish, the rhizodont, around 330 million years old, was discovered at Cocklawburn in 2007. Other branches of the Sarcopterygian family made the transition from water to land, which was one of the most significant events in vertebrate evolution. They became the ancestors of all four-limbed creatures, including humans. The rhizodont's evolutionary place is complex; its massive shoulder paddles have led some scientists to suggest that it was able to haul itself temporarily out of water. It became extinct 310 million years ago. The hashtag light-heartedly links it to another significant transition, that from analogue to digital in our own technological evolution.

BOOK II: INVISIBLE EVERYWHERE

Organic (96). Organic chemistry deals with carbon compounds, the basis of Life on Earth. Limestone and chalk are carbonates of calcium. Single-celled protozoa surrounded by protective calcium carbonate plates called 'coccoliths' play an important role in the carbon cycle, drawing down carbon dioxide from the atmosphere. They are the main constituent of chalk deposits. The poem picks up a line from 'Cocklawburn' (92). It and the chant which follows are part of the 'Susurrations' sequence. The chant echoes lines from 'Arguments' (68) in Part I.

The Website at the End of the World (98) is a response to the question, 'What would you place in your Imaginary Museum?' It was commissioned by the November Club for the 'Imaginary Museum of the North' at the Lit & Phil, Newcastle, in 2018.

Ingenious (99–111). This poem sequence began as an audio colla-boration, based on the words of a young robotics engineer, Jack Haworth, and the work of innovative sound designer Adam Fowler.

Jack is an engineer at Sellafield Ltd nuclear site in Cumbria. He specialises in robotics, using remotely operated vehicles for the exploration and mapping of contaminated areas of 'legacy waste', extremely hazardous to humans, to prepare for their eventual decommissioning. What initially interested me about his interview was his very matter-of-fact description of his work. It made me think about the use of autonomous systems elsewhere. I saw parallels between some of the remote sensing techniques he discussed, such as LiDAR (Light Detecting and Ranging), and those used in the extreme environment of Antarctica. I had already explored that subject in the sequence 'Under the Ice', which follows later in this book. Jack's interview gave me a starting-point from which to consider the idea of autonomous tools which extend human senses and activities, not only in hazardous places on Earth, but also in space. At the time of writing these poems in 2021, the NASA rover 'Perseverance' and helicopter 'Ingenuity' had just begun operating on Mars.

The word 'robotic' is derived from a word meaning 'slave'. I was interested in the language of control which Jack used: he talked of 'master-slave manipulators' and 'computer numerical control'. 'Control' is a key concept in computing, and one which I wanted to explore, as our world increasingly seems dominated by data-driven systems which impact on ideas of social freedom. I wanted to consider the sinister potential for social control inherent in data collection, 'truth' manipulation and generative artificial intelligence, and the choices we can still make to maintain freedom of thought and expression.

Collaboration was another strong theme of Jack's interview. I was interested in his emphasis on how teamwork brings multiple perspectives to a problem. I heard resonances between his ideas and ancient philosophical debates about mind and body, and between some of the engineering processes which Jack described and processes of nature. As Jack pointed out, both engineers and artists need to be inquisitive and creative problem-solvers. I agree: I have always found the distinction between the arts and sciences unhelpful. During the decade 2011-2021 much of my poetry was written in association with scientists, particularly with the late Peter Zinovieff, the composer of 'Under the Ice', whose work in the 1960s and 70s involved early experiments in machine learning for sound processing.

Jack's description of his work, and Zinovieff's early work, drew me towards metaphors based on overlapping models of complex systems: ecological, technological, biological, social and cognitive. Beneath such metaphors lies a cross-disciplinary approach called 'Cybernetics', defined by its originator Norbert Wiener as 'the science of control and communications in the animal and the machine'. Cybernetics is based on the idea of 'feedback', that the outcomes of actions should be inputs for future actions in the emergence of complex systems. This engineering process closely maps onto our understanding of biological evolution.

In the original podcast of 'Ingenious', producer Adam Fowler edited extracts from Jack's interview with Trevor Cox around the poem, and set the whole piece to his own haunting sound design, which was derived from sampled sounds from a servo mechanism. It can be found here: https://shows.acast.com/inventive-podcast/episodes/episode-five-jack-haworth   In this text version, I have arranged 'Ingenious' as a continuous poetic sequence in three loose sections, unified by metaphors and recurrent song-like choruses. Further notes on each section follow.

The first section of 'Ingenious', **Autonomous** (99-102), presents the theme of extending human senses and actions beyond the human body. Verse I introduces the idea. Verses II and III present examples of 'extreme environments'. The first, a visit to Mars, introduces the idea of Cybernetics, described above, which applies metaphors or models from the natural world to systems engineering. In verse III, the extreme environment is Jack's workplace, Sellafield's 'legacy' nuclear waste storage ponds. Verses IV and V then focus on Jack's work dealing with that hazardous waste using two different autonomous vehicles. The first of these is CARMA (Continuous Autonomous Radiometric Monitoring Assistant), a wheeled robot used for 3D mapping of radioactive contamination. The second is MIRRAX (Miniature Robot for Restricted Access Exploration), a reconfigurable, omnidirectional robot, carrying radiation sensors and light detecting and ranging equipment. Versatile enough to squeeze through a six-inch gap or to climb stairs, MIRRAX is used for nuclear decommissioning.

Section 2, **Space** (103-05) extends Jack's description of his work in extreme environments into outer space. Verse I, 'ADR' (Active Debris Removal), considers robots designed to collect junk in space. Many thousands of objects from past space missions remain in Earth orbit, creating a potential hazard to other spacecraft. Various robotic solutions have been proposed, and the European Space Agency is currently developing a new space servicing vehicle which may be capable of implementing some of these. Verse II reflects briefly on the language of robotics. Verses III and IV then consider two NASA Mars rovers which are still active in 2024. 'Curiosity' (which superseded three earlier Mars vehicles) landed in August 2012. The most recent rover, 'Perseverance', landed on 18 February 2021. Perseverance carried a small helicopter, 'Ingenuity', which sent back data to it between 19 April 2021 and 18 January 2024. The poem reflects on the human response to these complex autonomous operations.

Section 3, **Cybernetics** (106–11). The idea of Cybernetics, described above, is further developed in the closing section of the poem. 'Ingenious' explores the idea that the very survival of our species depends upon engineers. 'Anthropogenic' activities are balanced at a point where we might be engineering our own extinction, or our escape from it. One possibility is the potential development of human-machine hybrids. This is no longer science fiction: as I write, in February 2024, Elon Musk's Neuralink Corp. has just implanted the first computer interface into a human brain. Might we be at a transitional moment? The last part of 'Ingenious' explores this and other possibilities.

Verse IV, 'Moon' (107), considers autonomous vehicles surveying the Moon for future mining operations and human settlement. There is huge interest in commercial proposals to mine the Moon for three things: water, needed to sustain life in space, helium-3, required for nuclear fusion as a power source, and rare earth metals, vital to emerging technologies. In 2023 India and China had rovers active on the Moon, but India's rover has since reached the end of its life. At the time of writing, in February 2024, Japan has become the fifth country to land a spacecraft on the Moon. Meanwhile Intuitive Machines' 'Odysseus' has landed near the lunar South Pole, carrying scientific payloads on behalf of NASA. It is the first commercial spacecraft to make a lunar landing.

In verses V-IX (108-11), 'Ingenious' concludes with a reflection on the human place in nature, emphasising the physical body and its senses, human empathy and emotion, and the key roles that these play in conscious intelligence. Verses VI and VII touch on the sinister potential of artificial intelligence and intelligent automation for social control. At this stage, crucially, artificial intelligence is not yet conscious. The potential for creating conscious intelligence is highly debated. Some scientists believe that machine conscious-ness might be attained through a vast multiplicity of connections, simulating neural networks. Inspired by the fact that the word 'engineer' is derived from the Latin 'ingenium', which means an innate, natural quality – and from which we derive our words 'ingenuity' and 'genius' – the poem ends by suggesting that we should think positively. It emphasises that we still have choices. It suggests that freedom and hope may lie in the possibilities for collaboration between the immense reasoning powers of machines and the complexities of human consciousness, crucially embedded in the physical world. This is an exciting prospect for future generations.

Wave (112). The final poem from the 'Susurrations' sequence extends the biological and physical 'machine' analogies, tracing in Earth's ocean waves and the tiniest constituents of its ecosystems the 'machinery of star and galaxy'. All emanate from and operate within the same immutable laws of physics.

Under the Ice (113-24). The last sequence in the book explores the remote sensing techniques used to investigate the hidden landscapes beneath Antarctica's ice, to discern the movement of glaciers, and to understand more about Earth's changing climate. Intended for the non-scientist, it takes the reader or audience on a journey to an unseen world.

Like 'Ingenious', and many of the sequences in this collection, 'Under the Ice' began as a collaboration. Fittingly for a piece on remote sensing, that collaboration happened remotely, as the piece was researched and written during the Covid lockdowns of 2020-2021. I worked with electronic composer Peter Zinovieff, scientists from Northumbria University's Cold and Palaeo-Environments team, and NUSTEM's Exploring Extreme Environments programme, to create a half-hour performance for live voice, computer audio and satellite imagery. It was my final collaboration with Zinovieff. It premiered on Zoom, in an event hosted by the Wordsworth Trust, Grasmere, on 23 June 2021.

Antarctica is enormous, nearly twice the size of the continent of Australia. It is a desert, the coldest, driest, windiest place on Earth. It is almost entirely covered in an ice sheet, which averages over a mile in depth, and in some places reaches nearly three miles. Beneath this ice lie vast mountains, valleys, lakes and volcanoes, landscapes more difficult to visit than those which 'Ingenious' touches upon in outer space.

As the ice sheet flows outwards and downwards under the pressure of its own weight, glaciers form. They creep very slowly towards the ocean, where they extend into the sea as ice shelves. These stabilise the land ice, acting as buttresses. They are, however, vulnerable to warming water, and there have been several dramatic collapses in recent years, especially on the West Antarctic Peninsula. The science explored in 'Under the Ice' attempts to understand the mechanisms which drive these enormous processes. The poems concentrate in particular on Thwaites Glacier and Pine Island Glacier on the West Antarctic ice sheet, which flow into the Amundsen Sea. These two glaciers are particularly vulnerable to ice loss and potential collapse, and are crucial to the understanding of climate change.

Unseen (113). The first poem in the sequence presents an overview of Antarctica, the processes by which its ice sheets endlessly replenish themselves, and the hidden, inaccessible underworld of the continent's bedrock. Scientists studying glaciers observe Earth's smallest and largest phenomena: microscopic clues in the bedrock supply evidence of how a glacier advances or retreats over enormous timescales; air bubbles in ice cores reveal the composition of the atmosphere over hundreds of thousands of years; radar and satellite data supply information about the dynamics of the glacier and the ice sheet which feeds it.

Float (114). This poem examines the paradoxical nature of ice and its role on Earth. According to the British Antarctic Survey, around 60% of the world's total fresh water, and 90% of the world's surface fresh water, is held in the Antarctic ice sheet. If it was all to melt and return to its ice-free state of 90 million years ago, this would mean a 70 metre rise in global sea level.

Thwaites (114). Thwaites Glacier is a key to Antarctica's Western ice sheet. Its floating ice shelf acts as a precarious buttress, slowing its progress. Theoretical studies supported by observation investigate its vulnerability to potential collapse. In recent years, its flow has accelerated and its 'grounding line' – the boundary between the grounded ice sheet and the adjoining ice shelf – has retreated. Thwaites Glacier and Pine Island Glacier are closely monitored for their potential to raise sea levels.

Antarctica Without Its Ice (115). Sediment cores taken from the sea-bed near Pine Island Glacier show us that 90 million years ago the vast continent was ice-free and forested. Catastrophic climate change has happened many times in geological history. Scientists studying Antarctica's ice sheets are trying to understand more about the processes involved. As many scientists have pointed out, it is astonishing that for most of Earth's 4.5 billion year history its climate has been able to sustain a continuum of Life; but as Stephen Jay Gould argued in *Wonderful Life*, the rate of evolution is not steady. It is clear that complex ecologies, containing sophisticated organisms, emerge or re-emerge at times when more favourable conditions recur.

Five Eyes (116). Remote sensing techniques used to explore and measure Antarctica's rocks include satellite imaging such as Landsat, aerial photogrammetry by plane and drone, and LiDAR (Light Detecting and Ranging), which can very accurately measure movement. Antarctica's rocky world, for so long hidden a mile or more beneath ice sheets, can now be mapped and 'made visible' by means of ice-penetrating radar, deployed from a plane, drone, or from a snowmobile on the ground. A 'fifth eye', the human one, interprets the information gathered by these methods.

Cosmogenic Nuclide (117). Beryllium-10 is a Cosmogenic Nuclide used in dating techniques to determine the rate of the ice sheet's thinning and recession. It forms as a result of bombardment of the rock's surface by cosmic rays which originate from high-energy supernova explosions. Bombardment only occurs when the rock is exposed. Beryllium-10 is used to measure the age of moraines and glacially-eroded bedrock surfaces, and the extent of past ice sheet cover, providing evidence of the glacier's advance and retreat over vast timescales. The 'trimline' marks the maximum vertical extent of a past glaciation.

Basal Shear (118). 'Basal Shear' is a term used to describe the interaction of glacier and bedrock. Glaciers flow downhill in response to their driving stresses, which arise from the weight of the ice and gravity. Basal Shear is the stress which causes the ice to deform and the glacier to flow. Basal shear stress varies across the glacier bed because glaciers flow over highly uneven surfaces, varying in temperature, roughness and softness.

Invisible Mending (119). This poem is a response to research by Dr Kate Winter, former Baillet Latour Antarctic Fellow at Northumbria University, who was based at Princess Elisabeth Research Station in December 2018 and 2019. Kate's research centred on iron-rich sediments, carried by glaciers from inland areas of Antarctica to the Southern Ocean, which are thought to encourage the growth of microscopic phytoplankton. These in turn help to reduce carbon dioxide in Earth's atmosphere. As ice sheets thin in response to climate change, sediment delivery and production could increase, and with them absorption of carbon dioxide through the phyto-plankton's photosynthesis. It is uplifting to hear this positive story amid so much bad news about the climate. 'Nunataks' are the tops of mountains appearing above the ice as rocky points. The 'grounding line' is the boundary where the grounded ice sheet adjoins the floating ice shelf.

Ice Core (120). Deep ice cores drilled from Antarctica contain bubbles of air up to 800,000 years old, a stratigraphic record of Earth's atmosphere and climate change over at least eight glacial and inter-glacial cycles. According to the British Antarctic Survey, these ice cores show that atmospheric carbon dioxide levels are currently nearly 50% higher than before the Industrial Revolution, and that the magnitude and rate of this increase is almost certainly unprecedented over 800,000 years. This poem places that long record against a much greater geological timespan.

Waves (120). This poem, like the last in the 'Susurrations' sequence (112), reflects on wave-forms on vastly different scales, from the immense planetary 'waves' of glaciation, to the tiny radio waves which humans use to penetrate the ice and map its bedrock. Basic multicellular organisms survived a period of intense glaciation which ended around 635 million years ago. More complex Life has evolved on Earth in the relatively warmer conditions since then, which have included within them waves of ice ages and much warmer periods. Also within that time there have been five major extinction events. It appears that large-scale changes, such as dramatic warming or cooling, and mass extinctions, in turn open up space for evolution. This is a poet's reflection on those successive 'waves'.

Numerical Ice Sheet Modelling (121). Ice sheet models use numerical methods to simulate the evolution, dynamics and thermodynamics of ice sheets. The algorithms used in such modelling, and the human interpretation of physical and remote sensing data fed into them, are vital to the understanding of climate change. 'Firn' is granular snow on the upper part of a glacier, not yet compressed into ice.

Melt (122). A final reflection on the planetary forces, such as atmospheric and oceanic currents, which connect the smallest and largest phenomena. Warm ocean currents are 'hauled south', in the immense cyclical processes referred to in the 'Susurrations of the Sea' poems. When these warm currents reach Antarctica they undercut ice buttresses like the ice shelf at Thwaites Glacier, weakening them, with potentially disastrous consequences for the Western ice sheet.

Remote Sensing (123). The final poem in this sequence, and in the book, returns to remote sensing and information-gathering techniques, reflecting in awe and wonder that human consciousness is able to gather and interpret that information. While ice is ubiquitous in the Universe, the ability to understand it seems vanishingly rare – as far as we know, unique to our species and our astonishing, self-regulating planet.

ACKNOWLEDGEMENTS

My thanks to the following people, publications and organisations, for making these poems possible, and for giving them their first audience.

'Tinkers' Fires' was first published in *The Valley Press Anthology of Prose Poetry*, ed. Anne Caldwell and Oz Hardwick (Valley Press, 2019).

The poems between pages 20 and 27 were commissioned by the National Trust for the People's Landscape project, New Writing North and Durham Book Festival 2019. They were first published, together with poems by Phoebe Power and artwork by Rose Ferraby, in *Sea Change* (Guillemot Press, 2021). With thanks to Phoebe and Rose, and to Dr Luke Thompson. Special thanks to Horden Youth and Community Centre; the Head, staff and years 5 and 6 children of Cotsford Junior School, Horden; Ellin Hare and Nicola Balfour of the Barn at Easington; Easington Brownies and Guides; and artist Sharon Bailey and Hawthorn Dene Heritage Project. 'Coastal Erosion' was later published in *Earth Days Numbered*, ed. Joy Howard (Grey Hen Press, 2021) and 'Painted Ladies' in *The National Trust Book of Nature Poems*, ed. Deborah Alma (2023).

'Hermeneutics' was commissioned by Dr Sandra Raban for *The First Women, TH Women40* (Trinity Hall, Cambridge, 2016). 'Wooden Doll' was written for *The Wooden Dollies of North Shields*, ed. Keith Armstrong and Peter Dixon (Northern Voices Community Projects, 2018). 'Sa'at' was written for *Herring Our Joy*, a CD of songs about the herring industry, produced by Mary Garvey, 2021. 'Old Low Light' and 'Shields Gut' were written for *Tyne Anew*, ed. Keith Armstrong and Peter Dixon (NVCP, 2019). 'Old Low Light' was inspired by Sheila Hirsch, and set to music and sung by Celia Bryce.

The poems between pages 35 and 51 were nearly all commissioned by Amble Development Trust as part of *The Bird Roads* audio podcast series, a collaboration with Geoff Sample for the Bord Waalk sculpture trail and app (2023). The exceptions are 'Passage Migrants', which first appeared in *Woven Landscapes*, ed. Deborah Gaye (Avalanche Books, 2016), and 'Cubby', which was commended in the Winchester Poetry Prize competition 2018 and published in the prizewinners' anthology, *The Blaze in Father's Breath* (Winchester, 2018). The Bird Roads project was funded by the Coastal

Communities Fund, Arts Council England and Northumberland County Council.

'Sandylowper' was first published online in *Prac Crit*, edition 7, 2016. 'A Lang Way Hyem' was commissioned by BBC Radio 4 as part of the *Conversations on a Bench* series produced by Adam Fowler and Anna Scott-Brown (Overtone Productions, 2016). The interviews from which these extracts are adapted were conducted by Anna Scott-Brown and edited by Adam Fowler. With grateful thanks to Anna, Adam, and all the interviewees. Excerpts from this poem were first published in *Wild Fish* (Salmon and Trout Conservation, 2021) and *Forecast* (Books by the Sea, 2021).

'Goldcrests' was first published in *Quartet, the Four Seasons*, ed. Deborah Gaye (Avalanche Books, 2018). 'The Long Line' was commissioned by Historic England as part of an audio collaboration with Peter Zinovieff for the *Immortalised* exhibition in London, 2018. With grateful thanks to John Dixon and the interviewees from my archive for their part in the audio version of this piece.

'A Hut a Byens' and 'The Tide Clock' were commissioned by Newcastle Centre for the Literary Arts as part of the *Accessing Aidan* project, 2021. With thanks to John Challis and Jessica Turner. 'The Fulmar' was first published in *Pendulum: the poetry of dreams*, ed. Deborah Gaye (Avalanche, 2008). It subsequently appeared on the Irish State Examinations Commission English Junior Certificate Higher Level, paper 2, 2015.

The poems between pages 78 and 93 were commissioned in 2017 by Peregrini Lindisfarne Landscape Partnership, and first published in *Many Hands*, alongside photographs by Jose Snook. 'Anonymous' was later published in *Reflected Light*, ed. Joy Howard (Grey Hen Press, 2020). With thanks to Jose, Ros Duncan of Peregrini Partnership, Northumberland Coast AONB, Ian Hall (publisher), geologist Ian Kille, archaeologist Richard Carlton, historian Jessica Turner, Islanders Richard Patterson, Ralph Wilson and Mary Gunn, and to the many volunteers who took part in the Peregrini projects.

'The Website at the End of the World' was commissioned by the November Club for the Imaginary Museum of the North at the Lit and Phil, Newcastle, 2018, and appeared in the Lit and Phil's members' newsletter. 'Ingenious' was commissioned in 2021 by Overtone Productions and the University of Salford for the *Inventive Podcast* series. With thanks to Adam Fowler, Anna Scott-Brown, interviewer Professor Trevor Cox and interviewee Jack Haworth. Colleagues at Northumbria University's NUSTEM developed additional educational resources. 'How the Fishes Listen', 'Ingredients', 'Off Beadnell Point', 'Arguments', 'Organic' and 'Wave' were commissioned for *Susurrations of the Sea*, BBC Radio 4, produced by Julian May, December 2022. Julian has been a friend, collaborator and important commissioner of my work for a quarter of a century. I can't thank him enough.

'Under the Ice' was commissioned by NUSTEM (Northumbria University), as part of the *Exploring Extreme Environments* project, funded by the Science and Technology Facilities Council. It was my final collaboration with the late electronic composer Peter Zinovieff, and premiered online as part of the *Go to the Poets* series organised by the Wordsworth Trust, Grasmere, on 23 June 2021. Peter had been my friend and collaborator for nearly three decades. I would like to thank his family, especially his widow Jenny, and daughter Sofka, for their invaluable friendship and support. Thanks also to Professor John Woodward and Dr Kate Winter (Geography and Environmental Sciences, Northumbria University), and especially Dr Carol Davenport and all at NUSTEM for advice and support throughout the making of this piece. Additional thanks to Professor Philip Samartzis (RMIT University, Melbourne) and Chris Watson for their recordings of Antarctic glaciers, from which Peter selected samples for his composition. 'Invisible Mending' was selected for the 2020 Antarctic Poetry Competition. It was first published in *Planet in Peril*, ed. Isabelle Kenyon (Fly on the Wall Press, 2019), and in *Different Days,* ed. Joy Howard (Grey Hen Press, 2022).

To every one of my friends, collaborators, funders and publishers named above I owe a huge debt of gratitude. Thank you all. Thanks to Harry Beamish, Carol Davenport, Ian Kille and Martin Pacey for correcting errors in my notes. The remaining mistakes are of course all my own work. Thanks to Mark Cocker for providing inspiration for particular poems in Book I. Heartfelt thanks to Neil Astley and everyone at Bloodaxe Books, who have championed my work since the late 1980s. Special thanks to my beloved parents, Ian and Joan, who died within months of each other while this book was in preparation. Thank you for your endless love and support over 63 years.

Finally, special thanks to Paul Kenny for his wonderful cover image, 'Mapping the Strandline – Sea, Metal, Plastic, 2016'. Paul first contacted me when he heard some of the Peregrini Lindisfarne poems in 2017 and we felt an immediate connection through our work. He writes: 'This image was made with sixteen selectively cut fragments of plastic 7Up bottles found over three years on beaches in the west of Ireland, probably all brought by the Gulf Stream from the east coast of North America. The rust staining was made from a large washer found on the beach at Belderg in Mayo. Seawater collected at Belderg was seeped under for about two months.' Thank you, Paul, for your inspirational images and for giving *Rhizodont* such a striking presence in the world.

BIOGRAPHICAL NOTE

Katrina Porteous was born in Aberdeen, grew up in Co. Durham, and has lived on the Northumberland coast since 1987. She read History at Cambridge and afterwards studied in the USA on a Harkness Fellowship. Many of the poems in her first collection, *The Lost Music* (Bloodaxe Books, 1996), focus on the Northumbrian fishing community, about which Katrina has also written in prose in *The Bonny Fisher Lad* (The People's History, 2003). Katrina often writes in Northumbrian dialect, and has recorded her long poem, *The Wund an' the Wetter*, on CD with piper Chris Ormston (Iron Press, 1999). In recognition of her work on dialect and fishing, she is President of the Northumbrian Language Society and of the Coble and Keelboat Society. Katrina received an Arts Foundation Fellowship in 2003. Her second full-length collection from Bloodaxe, *Two Countries* (2014), was shortlisted for the Portico Prize for Literature in 2015.

Katrina has been involved in many collaborations with other artists, including public art for Seaham, Co. Durham, with sculptor Michael Johnson, and two books with maritime artist James Dodds, *Longshore Drift* (Jardine Press, 2005) and *The Blue Lonnen* (Jardine Press, 2007). She has collaborated on a book about the Durham Coast, *Sea Change*, alongside poet Phoebe Power and artist Rose Ferraby (Guillemot Press, 2021). With wildlife sound recordist Geoff Sample she has created a series of podcasts for The Bord Waalk sculpture trail, Amble (2023). Katrina often performs with musicians, including Chris Ormston, Alistair Anderson and (at Dartington International Music Festival 2018 and 2019) Alexis Bennett. Her work has been set by John Casken for the National Youth Choir (*Uncertain Sea*, 2014) and by Kristina Arakelyan for the BBC Proms (*Whin Lands*, 2023).

Katrina is particularly known for her radio-poetry, much of it produced by Julian May. One of these poems, *The Refuge Box*, is now part of a permanent installation in Lindisfarne Priory Museum, alongside a painting by Olivia Lomenech Gill. Another, *Horse*, with electronic music by Peter Zinovieff, first performed at Sage Gateshead for the BBC Radio 3 Free Thinking Festival 2011, is published as an artists' book and CD, with prints by Olivia Lomenech Gill (Windmillsteads Books, 2014). A further audio collaboration with

Zinovieff, *The Long Line*, was selected for Historic England's *Immortalised* exhibition in London in 2018.

Katrina's third full-length collection, *Edge* (Bloodaxe Books, 2019), draws on three collaborations commissioned for performance in Life Science Centre Planetarium, Newcastle, between 2013 and 2016, with multi-channel electronic music by Zinovieff: *Field*, *Sun* and *Edge*. *Sun* was part of NUSTEM's Imagining the Sun project (Northumbria University, 2016). *Edge*, a poem in four moons incorporating sounds collected from space missions, was broadcast as a *Poetry Please Special* on BBC Radio 4 in 2013.

In 2021 Katrina received a Cholmondeley Award from the Society of Authors. Her final collaboration with Zinovieff, also for NUSTEM and Northumbria University, was *Under the Ice*, which premiered that year. The text is included in her fourth poetry book from Bloodaxe, *Rhizodont*, which was published in 2024. Katrina is currently working on a new prose book about Northumbrian fishing communities.